RIGHTLY RELATED

Going Deeper In Your Relationship With Jesus

Joel R. Stroud

ACKNOWLEDGEMENTS

It will be obvious to many readers that the author has been influenced by devotional writers and proponents of what is sometimes known as "the deeper life" movement. Of note among those who have impacted the writer through their works are Andrew Murray, E. M. Bounds, A. W. Tozer, Oswald Chambers, Ian Thomas, Adrian Rogers, L. E. Maxwell, Manley Beasley, Ron Dunn, and Henry Blackaby. Their writings and messages are highly recommended to readers who long to experience a deeper intimacy with Jesus. Of special significance is the work of Henry Blackaby entitled *Experiencing God*, which has been foundational to the author's understanding of a relationship with Christ.

Appreciation is extended to the author's brother, Dan Stroud, Jr. and good friend, Bob Josey, for their suggestions regarding content, organization, and clarity. The writer is also deeply indebted to his niece, Dr. April Stroud Roberts, for proofing the manuscript.

Finally, recognition is due Pastor Danny Hall and Pastor Dan Crow, two men of God, who took the author aside many years ago and "explained to him the way of God more accurately."

CONTENTS

PREFACE

Salvation is more than praying "the Sinner's Prayer," being baptized, joining a church, or trying to be a good person. Salvation is a relationship with Jesus Christ that is real and personal. Humanly speaking, it begins with an introduction to Jesus, i.e., when you invite Him into your heart and receive Him as your personal Savior. It is followed by a continuing walk with Him in deepening knowledge and intimacy.

Due to the historically strong emphasis on evangelism among conservatives, most churches have no shortage of members who have taken the first step of receiving Christ as their Savior. However, they have often not been taught how to follow Jesus daily as an obedient disciple. As a consequence of not going deeper, their relationship with Christ is not very satisfying. They are often inconsistent in Bible study and church attendance, lack assurance of salvation, power to resist sin, courage to share their faith, or concern for kingdom advancement.

It is the writer's conviction that the present blight upon western Christianity can be traced to a failure of the church to teach and of Christians to understand the nature, privileges, and responsibilities of a relationship with Jesus. The Biblical truths and principles presented in this volume are offered to the reader with the firm belief that if believers can get it right at the Source and remain rightly related to Jesus, He will produce much fruit that remains for the glory of God.

Joel R. Stroud
July 2018

Romans 3:23 Man is a sinner.

Ro 6:23 Sin separates man from God.

Ro 5:8 Jesus died as our sin substitute

Eph 2:8-9 Salvation is by God's grace
through faith, never by works.

1- RELATIONSHIP *w/ Jesus*

A good place to begin this investigation is to consider the question...

Where did relationship begin?

The concept of relationship predates the human family. Before the creation of mankind, the triune God existed from eternity past. Although we know little of what transpired in the eons of former ages, we can infer that the Father, Son, and Holy Spirit existed and delighted in one another within the holy fellowship of the Godhead. Anticipating His return to the Father, Jesus spoke of Their mutual glory in His priestly intercession in John 17.

> John 17:5 And now, O Father, glorify Me together with Yourself (i.e. in your presence, beside you), <u>with the glory which I had with You before the world was</u>.

> John 17:22 And the glory which You gave Me I have given them, <u>that they may be one just as We are one</u>:

> John 17:24 Father, I desire that they also whom You gave Me may be with Me where I am, that

they may behold My glory which You have given Me; <u>for You loved Me before the foundation of the world</u>.

The members of the Godhead shared fully, equally, and eternally the unique glory (i.e. the perfections of deity) which belongs to God and God alone. Each one possessed complete and thorough knowledge of the others, and They related to each other in perfect love, unity, equality, righteousness, joy, etc.

In the book of Genesis, we learn God created mankind as an expression of His unique glory.

> Gen. 1:26 Then God said, Let <u>Us make man in Our image, according to Our likeness</u>; let them have dominion over the fish of the sea, over the birds of the air, and over the cattle, over all the earth and over every creeping thing that creeps on the earth. Gen. 1:27 <u>So God created man in His *own* image; in the image of God He created him; male and female He created them</u>.

First, God created the man, and then we read...

> Gen. 2:18 And the Lord God said, *It is* not good that man should be alone; <u>I will make him a helper comparable (i.e. perfectly suited) to him</u>.

To properly reflect the glory of the Holy Trinity, it was necessary for God to create a partner and helper for Adam.

The first couple ruled over the works of God's hands and lived in relationship with each other. They shared the same *essence*.

> Gen. 2:23 And Adam said: <u>This *is* now bone of my bones and flesh of my flesh</u>; she shall be called Woman, because she was taken out of Man.

Adam and Eve reflected the *unity* of the Godhead.

> Gen. 2:24 Therefore a man shall leave his father and mother and be joined to his wife, <u>and they shall</u>

become one flesh.

The man and his wife enjoyed complete *openness* and *acceptance* in their relationship.

> Gen. 2:25   And they were both naked, the man and
> his wife, and were not ashamed.

From the "Book of Beginnings," we also learn that the relationship they enjoyed with their Creator and with each other was corrupted when they ate of the forbidden fruit. The evidence of the broken relationship soon became apparent. Adam and Eve tried to avoid accountability for their wrongdoing.

> Gen. 3:8   And they heard the sound of the Lord God
> walking in the garden in the cool of the day, and
> Adam and his wife hid themselves from the presence
> of the Lord God among the trees of the garden.

Our first parents were ashamed of their nakedness, but not of their disobedience.

> Gen. 3:10   So he said, I heard Your voice in the
> garden, and I was afraid because I was naked; and I
> hid myself.
> Gen. 3:11   And He said, Who told you that you
> *were* naked?   Have you eaten from the tree of which
> I commanded you that you should not eat?

When confronted with their sin, Adam and Eve became defensive and even implied that God was somehow at fault.

> Gen. 3:12   Then the man said, The woman whom
> You gave *to be* with me, she gave me of the tree,
> and I ate.
> Gen. 3:13   And the Lord God said to the woman,
> What *is* this you have done? The woman said, The
> serpent deceived me, and I ate.

It is clear from Scripture that relationship is fundamental to the nature of God and the human family. The Bible faithfully records the history of our predecessors in terms of their relationships with God and with one another. Moreover, even in our fallen state, it cannot be denied that people still need and long for the satisfaction, security, and significance derived from personal relationships with each other.

There are several levels of relationship. There is *acquaintance* as with someone you have just met. There is *association* as with someone with whom you work. A closer level of relationship would be *comradeship* as with those who serve in the military. Deeper still is *friendship* as with a buddy, pal, and confidant. *Family* connections are usually the deepest of all human relationships.

The greatest intimacy two people can experience is that of husband and wife within the relationship of marriage as God ordained it. This relationship involves a level of sharing, vulnerability, intimacy, and pleasure deeper than any other. In the Scriptures, the marriage relationship is described as *knowing* and *being known* of another, and the expression is an idiom signifying sexual intimacy between a man and his wife.

> Gen. 4:1 <u>Now Adam knew Eve his wife, and she conceived and bore Cain</u>, and said, I have acquired a man from the Lord.

The Bible also describes salvation in terms of intimate knowledge and uses the same word from two different perspectives--our knowing Jesus and the Father...

> John 17:3 And this is eternal life, <u>that they may know You</u>, the only true God, <u>and Jesus Christ</u> whom You have sent.

...and our being known of God and His Son.

> Gal. 4:9 But now after <u>you have known God</u>, or rather <u>are known by God</u>, how *is it that* you turn again to the weak and beggarly elements, to which you desire again to be in bondage?

4

Mt. 7:22 Many will say to Me in that day, Lord, Lord, have we not prophesied in Your name, cast out demons in Your name, and done many wonders in Your name?

Mt. 7:23 And then I will declare to them, <u>I never knew you</u>; depart from Me, you who practice lawlessness (i.e. work iniquity)!

God is all about relationship. It is fundamental to His nature as the triune God. He created all of us to live in relationship— marriage, family, friendships, the body of Christ, etc. Furthermore, God desires a relationship with you and me, and He wants us to know and experience Him.

This book is for everyone who desires to go deeper in their understanding of what it means to be rightly related to Jesus, so as we begin this study, would you honestly consider the following questions? Do you have a relationship with Jesus that is real and personal? Do you sometimes struggle with doubts or do you have a confident assurance of your salvation?

2- DIMESIONS OF RELATIONSHIP

Life can be described as a series of relationships, and a good life, a fulfilling life, is the result of good relationships. Some people are good at relationships, while others are rotten at them. Sometimes, people stay in failing relationships because they have no other choice, or they don't want to feel like a failure or lose someone's approval. Others go through life carelessly leaving a trail of broken relationships—broken relationships with parents, broken marriages, broken relationships with children, friends, co-workers, employers—you name it.

How are your relationship skills? Just because you are on speaking terms with someone doesn't mean you have a healthy relationship with that person. You don't have to be fighting with your spouse or in divorce court to be failing in your marriage. Similarly, you don't have to be slacking in your church attendance, stealing from your neighbor, or worshipping an idol to be failing in your relationship with Jesus. In fact, you can be like the scribes and Pharisees.

> Mt. 23:28 Even so <u>you also outwardly appear righteous to men, but inside you are full of hypocrisy and lawlessness (i.e. iniquity)</u>.

You can outwardly exhibit moral behavior without a right relationship with Jesus, but you cannot be rightly related to Jesus without godly behavior.

In this chapter, we will discover more of what it means to have a relationship with Christ. Let's begin by asking...

What are the dimensions of a personal, love relationship with Jesus?

With a little research, you will discover that experts recognize approximately nine dimensions of a healthy, personal relationship. Consider the following list and clarifications.

- Accessibility—You typically need to be in close proximity to have a personal relationship. Long distance romances don't usually work out.
- Communication—You must talk to each other. People who don't communicate don't know each other. It is possible to be married and remain a stranger to your spouse without honest, meaningful communication.
- Intimacy—There must be self-disclosure. You don't share your feelings, values, dreams, hurts, disappointments, etc., with just anyone. In the marital relationship, you not only share your heart, but you enjoy sexual intimacy as well.
- Love—There must not only be affection and passion but commitment also. Loyalty and faithfulness are essential to lasting relationships.
- Fellowship—Someone has humorously defined fellowship as two fellows in the same ship. There must be shared values, purposes, goals, experiences, etc. If two people are not going in the same direction in life, they have little basis for a relationship.
- Appreciation—There must be admiration and approval expressed by those in the relationship. Compliments and expressions of appreciation are always welcomed and needful. *praise*

7

✓ • Responsibility—Irresponsible behavior can kill a relationship. Consequently, there must be a willingness on both parts to be accountable for inappropriate or hurtful conduct.

✓ • Trust—People in relationship must be able to trust each other, or it will not last. Distrust, suspicion, fear, and betrayal can destroy a relationship.

✓ • Transparency—For a healthy relationship, there must be honesty in thought, word, deed, attitude, and motive (no deception, no half-truths, no hypocrisy).

Incidentally, if you want to improve your relational skills, these are good ways to evaluate yourself.

Now, consider these same aspects of relationship in light of what Scripture says about how Jesus relates to us.

Accessibility—Jesus is accessible and approachable to us.

> Mt. 11:28 <u>Come to Me, all *you* who labor and are heavy laden (i.e. burdened down), and I will give you rest.</u>
> Mt. 11:29 Take My yoke upon you and learn from Me, for I am gentle and lowly in heart, and you will find rest for your souls.
>
> Acts 17:26 And He has made from one blood every nation of men to dwell on all the face of the earth, and has determined their preappointed times and the boundaries of their dwellings,
> Acts 17:27 So that they should seek the Lord, in the hope that they might grope for Him and find Him, <u>though He is not far from each one of us;</u>
> Acts 17:28 <u>For in Him we live and move and have our being,</u> as also some of your own poets have said, For we are also His offspring.

Communication—Jesus talks to us.

> John 10:27 <u>My sheep hear My voice,</u> and I know them, and they follow Me:

8

He listens to us when we talk to Him.

> Mt. 7:7 <u>Ask</u>, and it will be given to you; <u>seek</u>, and you will find; <u>knock</u>, and it will be opened to you. Mt. 7:8 <u>For everyone who asks receives, and he who seeks finds, and to him who knocks it will be opened</u>.

Intimacy—Jesus is intimate with us and we with Him.

He knows us and we know Him.

> John 10:14 I am the good shepherd; and <u>I know My *sheep*, and am known by My own</u>.

He tells us what He is thinking.

> 1 Cor. 2:16 For who has known the mind of the Lord, that He may instruct Him? But <u>we have the mind of Christ</u>.

Love—Jesus is committed to us.

> Rom. 8:38 For I am persuaded that neither death nor life, nor angels nor principalities nor powers, nor things present nor things to come,
> Rom. 8:39 Nor height nor depth, nor any other created thing, <u>shall be able to separate us from the love of God which is in Christ Jesus our Lord</u>.

He consoles us in our pain.

> 2 Cor. 1:3 Blessed *be* the God and Father of our Lord Jesus Christ, the Father of mercies and God of all comfort,
> 2 Cor. 1:4 <u>Who comforts us in all our tribulation</u>, that we may be able to comfort those who are in any trouble, <u>with the comfort with which we ourselves are comforted by God</u>.

Jesus empathizes and sympathizes.

Isa. 63:8 For He said, Surely they *are* My people, children *who* will not lie. So He became their Savior.

Isa. 63:9 <u>In all their affliction He was afflicted</u>, and the Angel of His Presence saved them; in His love and in His pity He redeemed them; and He bore them and carried them all the days of old.

He bears our burdens and cares for us.

1 Pet. 5:6 Therefore humble yourselves under the mighty hand of God, that He may exalt you in due time,

I Pet 5:7 <u>Casting all your care upon Him; for He cares for you</u>.

He is jealous, but not envious of us.

Ex. 34:13 But you shall destroy their altars, break their *sacred* pillars, and cut down their wooden images

Ex. 34: 14 (For you shall worship no other god, <u>for the Lord, whose name *is* Jealous, *is* a jealous God</u>),

Rev. 3:19 <u>As many as I love, I rebuke and chasten</u>: Therefore be zealous, and repent.

Jesus wants to share our tomorrows.

John 17:24 Father, <u>I desire that they also whom You gave Me may be with Me where I am</u>, that they may behold My glory which You have given Me; for You loved Me before the foundation of the world.

Fellowship—Jesus shares His life with us.

We go places together.

Josh. 1:9 Have I not commanded you? Be strong and of good courage; do not be afraid, nor be dismayed, <u>for the Lord your God *is* with you wherever you go</u>.

We spend time together.

> Heb. 13:5 Let your conduct be without covetousness; be content with such things as you have. For He Himself has said, <u>I will never leave you nor forsake you</u>.

We do things together.

> 1 Cor. 3:9 <u>For we are God's fellow workers</u>; you are God's field, *you are* God's building.

Appreciation—Jesus rejoices in our company.

> Pro. 3:12 For whom the LORD loves He corrects; just as a father *corrects* the son *in whom* <u>he delights</u>.

He appreciates and affirms us.

> Rom. 8:16 <u>The Spirit Himself bears witness with our spirit, that we are the children of God</u>:

Responsibility—Jesus is patient with us.

> 2 Pet. 3:9 The Lord is not slack (i.e. slow, careless) concerning *His* promise, as some count slackness, but is <u>longsuffering toward us</u>, not willing that any should perish but that all should come to repentance.

Jesus is not pushy, insisting on His rights.

> Rev. 3:20 <u>Behold, I stand at the door and knock. If anyone hears My voice and opens the door</u>, I will come in to him and dine with him, and he with Me.

He is considerate and thoughtful.

> 1 Cor. 10:13 No temptation has overtaken you except such as is common to man; <u>but God *is* faithful, who will not allow you to be tempted beyond what you are able</u>, but with the temptation

11

will also make the way of escape, that you may be able to bear it.

Jesus is kind and forbearing with us.

> Rom. 2:4 Or do you despise the riches of His goodness, forbearance, and longsuffering, not knowing that the goodness of God leads you to repentance?

He always keeps our best in view.

> Rom. 8:28 And we know that all things work together for good to those who love God, to those who are the called according to *His* purpose.

Trust—Jesus trusts us with His honor and reputation.

> John 17:9 I pray for them. I do not pray for the world but for those whom You have given Me, for they are Yours.
> John 17:10 And all Mine are Yours, and Yours are Mine, and I am glorified in them.

He trusts us with His interests and concerns.

> Mt. 28:19 Go therefore and make disciples of all the nations, baptizing them in the name of the Father and of the Son and of the Holy Spirit,

Transparency—Jesus is the God of truth.

> 1 John 5:20 And we know that the Son of God has come and has given us an understanding, that we may know Him who is true; and we are in Him who is true, in His Son Jesus Christ. This is the true God and eternal life.

> John 14:6 Jesus said to him, I am the way, the truth, and the life. No one comes to the Father except through Me.

He is forthright, truthful and honest—no hypocrisy or deception.

John 14:2 In My Father's house are many mansions;
If *it were* not *so,* I would have told you. I go to
prepare a place for you.

Given the aspects of relationship and what the Bible says
about how Jesus relates to us, does this describe your relationship
to Him? Is this how you experience Jesus?

- Is He accessible and approachable, or does He seem distant
  and faraway?
- Do you daily draw near to Jesus through prayer and Bible
  study?
- Does He talk to you, and do you talk to Him throughout the
  day?
- Is He sharing His heart with you, and are you sharing yours
  with Him?
- Does Jesus console your pain, empathize and sympathize
  with your suffering, bear your burdens, and care for you?
- Is He jealous for your affection, and does He discipline
  your sin?
- Do you go where Jesus goes, do what He does, and spend
  time with Him daily?
- Are there times when you sense His admiration and
  approval?
- Do you regularly express your appreciation to Him?
- Is Jesus patiently, lovingly working all things together for
  your good?
- You trust Him, but is He trusting you with His business?
- Are you transparent with Him, and is He revealing His
  truth to you?

This is what a relationship with Jesus looks like. Is this how
you relate to Jesus? Does your relationship need some work? Are
you sure you have a relationship with Him?

3- GETTING STARTED

An important question to ask at this point is…

How do we establish a relationship with God?

The Bible teaches that God desires a relationship with every one of us. In his popular and excellent work, *Experiencing God*, Henry Blackaby expounded Seven Realities Of Experiencing God. Number 2 was "God pursues a continuing love relationship with you that is real and personal." He pointed out that in our natural, human state, we do not seek God on our own initiative.

> Rom. 3:10   As it is written: There is none righteous, no, not one;
> Rom. 3:11   There is none who understands; there is none who seeks after God.

At Caesarea Philippi, Jesus asked His disciples who men said that He was. They answered, "John the Baptist, Elijah, Jeremiah, or one of the prophets." When asked who they believed Him to be, Peter gave his famous confession, revealing God's activity in his life.

> Mt. 16:16   Simon Peter answered and said, You are the Christ, the Son of the living God.

14

> Matt. 16:17 Jesus answered and said to him, Blessed are you, Simon Bar-Jonah, for flesh and blood has not revealed this to you, but My Father who is in heaven.

The Bible teaches that God must take the initiative.

> John 6:44 No man can come to Me unless the Father who sent Me draws him; and I will raise him up at the last day.
> John 6:45 It is written in the prophets, And they shall all be taught by God. Therefore everyone who has heard and learned from the Father comes to Me.
>
> John 6:65 And he said, Therefore I have said to you that no one can come to Me unless it has been granted to him of My Father.

The Old Testament Scriptures reveal God pursuing relationships with mankind. God came seeking Adam and Eve even after they had sinned. The Lord came to Noah, Abraham, and Moses. The New Testament reveals the same divine initiative. Jesus sought out the twelve disciples and came to Paul on the Damascus road.

A relationship with God is established when we respond to the conviction of the Holy Spirit and receive Jesus as our personal Savior.

> John 1:11 He came to His own, and His own did not receive Him.
> John 1:12 But as many as received Him, to them He gave the right to become children of God, to those who believe in His name:

At the moment we trust Christ, we are born again by the Spirit of God on the basis of grace (i.e. God's unmerited favor) alone.

> John 1:13 Who were born, not of blood (Greek: *himaton*- bloods), nor of the will of the flesh, nor of the will of man, but of God.

In the preceding verse, *blood(s)* refers to animal sacrifices offered to God that could atone for or cover, but never take away sin.

> Lev. 17:11 <u>For the life of the flesh is in the blood</u>, and I have given it to you upon the altar to make atonement for your souls; <u>for it is the blood that makes atonement for the soul</u>.

> Heb. 10:4 For it is not possible that <u>the blood of bulls and of goats</u> could take away sins.

The *will of the flesh* alludes to the inadequacy of personal works of righteousness done to gain God's approval.

> Phil. 3:3 For we are the circumcision, who worship God in the Spirit, rejoice in Christ Jesus, and have no confidence in the flesh,
> Phil. 3:4 <u>Though I might also have confidence in the flesh</u>. If anyone else thinks he may have confidence <u>in the flesh</u>, I more so:
> Phil. 3:5 Circumcised the eighth day, of the stock of Israel, of the tribe of Benjamin, a Hebrew of the Hebrews; concerning the law, a Pharisee;
> Phil. 3:6 Concerning zeal, persecuting the church; concerning <u>the righteousness which is in the law, blameless</u>.

The *will of man* refers to human desire as when Abraham expressed his longing for Ishmael to be included in the line of covenant blessing.

> Gen. 17:18 And Abraham said to God, <u>Oh, that Ishmael might live before You</u>!
> Gen. 17:19 <u>Then God said: No, Sarah your wife shall bear you a son</u>, and you shall call his name Isaac: <u>I will establish My covenant with him</u> for an everlasting covenant, and with his descendants after him.

Salvation is the work of God, but it involves human cooperation. We must repent of our sins, believe the good news of

Jesus, and receive Him as Lord and Savior. However, all that God commands, He enables, and all that He requires, He supplies.

✝Our relationship with Jesus begins when we...

(1) *Obey God's command to repent.*

> Acts 17:30 Truly, these times of ignorance God overlooked, <u>but now (He) commands all men everywhere to repent,</u>

Repentance is not just regret or feeling sorry for sin. If you get ticketed for speeding, you would probably regret exceeding the limit, getting caught, and the expense of going to traffic court. However, if being fined for breaking the law does not stop you from speeding, you have not repented.

Repentance signifies a change in attitude and thinking that is so profound and fundamental that it alters the way we behave. John the Baptist came preaching repentance. Notice what he taught.

> Lk. 3:8 <u>Therefore bear fruits worthy of repentance,</u> and do not begin to say to yourselves, We have Abraham as *our* father. For I say to you that God is able to raise up children to Abraham from these stones.
>
> Lk. 3:10 So the people asked him, saying, <u>What shall we do then?</u>
> Lk. 3:11 He answered and said to them, <u>He who has two tunics, let him give to him who has none; and he who has food, let him do likewise.</u>
> Lk. 3:12 Then tax collectors also came to be baptized, and said to him, Teacher, what shall we do?
> Lk. 3:13 And he said to them, <u>Collect no more than what is appointed for you.</u>
> Lk. 3:14 Likewise the soldiers asked him, saying, And what shall we do? So he said to them, <u>Do</u>

not intimidate anyone or accuse falsely, and be
content with your wages.

(2) *Believing on Jesus* is also necessary to establish a relationship.

> Acts 16:30   And he brought them out and said, Sirs,
> what must I do to be saved?
> Acts 16:31   So they said, Believe on the Lord Jesus
> Christ, and you will be saved, you and your
> household.

Faith or belief is often misunderstood. Believing on Jesus is more than an optimistic attitude or mental agreement with the facts of the gospel. To believe means to trust, depend on, and commit yourself to Jesus.

Sometimes people are erroneously encouraged to "just believe" as if faith somehow exists independently of its object or its effects. However, faith does not exist in a vacuum. It requires an object. You don't just have faith. You have faith *in* someone or something. Furthermore, believing in Jesus means *taking Him at His word* and *acting on what He said*. Faith and faith alone is what saves, but actions or works demonstrate that faith is real.

> James 2:17   Thus also faith by itself, if it does not
> have works, is dead.

Faith that does not result in a change of behavior is not true, saving faith. Do not be misled: We are not saved *by works* or *by faith and works*. We are saved *by faith that works*. When we believe God, He births us into His family, and our obedience proves that our faith is genuine and we have truly been born again.

> 1 John 2:3   Now by this we know that we know
> Him, if we keep His commandments.
> 1 John 2:4   He who says, I know Him, and does not
> keep His commandments, is a liar, and the truth is
> not in him.

When we repent and believe, we are born again of the Spirit of God.

> John 3:5   Jesus answered, Most assuredly, I say to you, <u>unless one is born of water and the Spirit, he cannot enter the kingdom of God.</u>
> John 3:6   That which is born of the flesh is flesh, and that which is born of the Spirit is spirit.
> John 3:7   Do not marvel that I said to you, <u>You must be born again.</u>

Repentance and faith are both gifts of God, but they are our responsibility. Spiritual rebirth is God's part. When we believe the good news, we are born from above. The Spirit of God, who knows our hearts, unites with our human spirit, and we become one spirit with the Lord.

> 1 Cor. 6:17   But <u>he who is joined to the Lord is one spirit</u> *with Him.*

At the moment we trust Messiah Jesus, a radical transaction occurs, the effects of which continue to impact our lives forever.

* We have fellowship with the Father and the Son.

> 1 John 1:3   That which we have seen and heard we declare to you, that you also may have fellowship with us; and <u>truly our fellowship is with the Father and with His Son Jesus Christ.</u>

* We are children of God.

> 1 John 3:1   <u>Behold what manner of love the Father has bestowed on us, that we should be children of God</u>! Therefore the world does not know us, because it did not know Him.

* We are righteous, holy, blameless, and unreprovable in God's sight. As someone has said, "Not even the eye of omniscience can detect an imperfection in you."

> 2 Cor. 5:21   For He made Him who knew no sin *to be* sin for us, <u>that we might become the righteousness of God in Him.</u>

Col. 1:21   And you, who once were alienated and enemies in your mind by wicked works, yet now He has reconciled
Col. 1:22   In the body of His flesh through death, <u>to present you holy, and blameless, and above reproach in His sight</u>—

* We have eternal life as an immediate possession.

1 John 5:11   And this is the testimony: that <u>God has given us eternal life, and this life is in His Son.</u>
1 John 5:12   <u>He who has the Son has life</u>; he who does not have the Son of God does not have life.

* We are delivered from Satan's dominion and placed under the authority of Jesus Christ.

Col. 1:13   He has <u>delivered us from the power of darkness and conveyed us into the kingdom of the Son of His love,</u>

* We are indwelled by the Holy Spirit.

Rom. 8:11   But <u>if the Spirit of Him who raised Jesus from the dead dwells in you</u>, He who raised Christ from the dead will also give life to your mortal bodies <u>through His Spirit who dwells in you</u>.

1 John 4:13   By this we know that we abide in Him, and He in us, <u>because He has given us of His Spirit</u>.

* We have citizenship in God's kingdom.

Phil. 3:20   <u>For our citizenship is in heaven,</u> from which we also eagerly wait for the Savior, the Lord Jesus Christ,

* We are heirs of God and joint heirs with Christ of all things.

Rom. 8:16 The Spirit Himself bears witness with our spirit that we are children of God,

Rom. 8:17 <u>And if children, then heirs—heirs of God and joint heirs with Christ,</u> if indeed we suffer with *Him,* that we may also be glorified together.

* We are ambassadors of Christ.

2 Cor. 5:20 Now then, <u>we are ambassadors for Christ, as though God were pleading through us</u>: we implore *you* on Christ's behalf, be reconciled to God.

* We are authorized and empowered to continue Jesus' mission.

John 17:18 As You have sent me into the world, even so have <u>I also sent them into the world.</u>

By virtue of our spiritual rebirth, we become children of God, but we are newborn babes in Christ. Just as an individual progresses through different stages of maturity from infancy to adulthood, we must grow in the grace and knowledge of Jesus.

1 Pet. 2:2 <u>As newborn babes, desire the pure milk of the word, that you may grow thereby,</u>
1 Pet. 2:3 If indeed you have tasted that the Lord *is* gracious.

Conversion is not the end but the beginning of a journey through life with Jesus. This process is facilitated by gifted leaders in the church, who equip Christians to use their spiritual gifts to build up the body of Christ. It is in a local fellowship of spiritually minded, growing believers that we are best nurtured in the faith of Jesus and motivated toward Christian maturity.

Eph. 4:11 And He Himself gave some *to be* <u>apostles</u>, some <u>prophets</u>, some <u>evangelists</u>, and some <u>pastors</u> and <u>teachers,</u>
Eph. 4:12 <u>For the equipping of the saints for the work of ministry, for the edifying of the body of Christ,</u>
Eph. 4:13 <u>Till we all come to the unity of the faith</u> and of <u>the knowledge of the Son of God, to a perfect</u>

21

man, to the measure of the stature of the fullness of Christ;

That is why we are urged by the writer of Hebrews...

Heb. 10:24   And let us consider one another in order to stir up love and good works,
Heb. 10:25 Not forsaking the assembling of ourselves together, as *is* the manner of some, but exhorting *one another,* and so much the more as you see the Day approaching.

Have you received God's Son as your personal Savior and publically identified with Him through believers' baptism? Do you enjoy daily communion with Jesus through prayer and Bible study? Are you in regular fellowship with other Christians who are learning to follow Jesus as His disciples?

4- ROUTINE MAINTENANCE

Relationships require work; they don't just happen. They must be maintained by the parties involved, and that is especially true of our relationship with Jesus.

Sin is a reality for us personally and for the church corporately. John made that clear in his epistle.

> 1 John 1:8 <u>If we say that we have no sin, we deceive ourselves</u>, and the truth is not in us.

> 1 John 1:10 <u>If we say that we have not sinned, we make Him a liar</u>, and His word is not in us.

Sin has to do with breaking the commandments of God. Thayer's Greek Lexicon gives the meaning of sin (Greek: *hamartia*) as "that which is done wrong, sin, an offence, a violation of the divine law in thought or in act." The literal meaning is to "miss the mark." God's law declared,

> Ex. 20:3 You shall have no other gods before Me.
> Ex. 20:4 You shall not make for yourself a carved image...
> Ex. 20:7 You shall not take the name of the Lord

your God in vain…
Ex. 20:8 Remember the Sabbath day, to keep it holy.
Ex. 20:12 Honor your father and your mother…
Ex. 20:13 You shall not murder.
Ex. 20:14 You shall not commit adultery.
Ex. 20:15 You shall not steal.
Ex. 20:16 You shall not bear false witness…
Ex. 20:17 You shall not covet…

To do otherwise was to sin—miss the mark—by violating God's commandments.

Another aspect of human rebellion that is not as well understood is iniquity. Iniquity has more to do with the subtle attitudes of pride and independence that give rise to sin.

When King David took the wife of Uriah, he committed the sin of adultery, but what gave rise to his sin? It was not just sexual desire. He had more than enough wives to meet his needs. The more serious problem was the attitude of his heart, the mindset that since he was king and answerable to no other man, he could do as he pleased, even if it meant having someone murdered, taking his wife, and covering up the whole shameful ordeal. When we read his confession, we notice that David was careful to recognize both his sin and his iniquity.

> Ps. 32:5 I acknowledged my sin to You, and my iniquity have I not hidden. I said, I will confess my transgressions to the LORD; and You forgave the iniquity of my sin.

> Ps. 51:2 Wash me thoroughly from my iniquity, and cleanse me from my sin.

Isaiah revealed the basic meaning of iniquity in his prophecy of the "Suffering Servant" who would one day bear Israel's sin.

> Isa. 53:6 All we like sheep have gone astray; we have turned every one to his own way; and the LORD has laid on Him the iniquity of us all.

When we try to live life on our terms and do things *our way* rather than God's, we commit iniquity. Following are just a few examples of how we choose our ways over God's ways.

- Focusing on the physical and temporal while neglecting the spiritual and eternal.
- Seeking God in the crisis and forgetting Him in times of prosperity.
- Seeking to be served rather than laying down our lives to serve others.
- Taking credit for our accomplishments instead of giving glory to God.
- Bragging on our successes instead of letting others recognize our achievements.
- Doing our spiritual service for the sake of man and not God.
- Refusing correction instead of hearing reproof.
- Taking matters into our own hands instead of trusting our situation to God.
- Relying on our own thinking instead of seeking God's wisdom.
- Focusing on present gratification instead of future consequences.
- Trying to always maintain control and avoiding vulnerability.
- Holding grudges or retaliating rather than forgiving offenders.
- Indulging rather than denying ourselves.
- Hoarding our resources instead of being rich toward God.

The only way to avoid iniquity is to seek the Lord with our whole heart and keep His testimonies. As we obey God's word, we come to understand the right ways of responding that underlie His commandments, and we are kept from iniquity.

> Ps. 119:2 Blessed *are* those who keep His testimonies, *and that* seek Him with the whole heart. Ps. 119:3 They also do no iniquity: they walk in His ways.

Although it is impossible for those who know Jesus to remain in a lifestyle of habitual disobedience, there are occasions of sin and iniquity that happen to every Christian. We have been born again of the Spirit of God, but we still live in a fallen world. Satan entices us through desires for fleshly gratification, the appeal of material possessions, and the desire for self-exaltation.

> 1 John 2:16 For all that *is* in the world—the lust of
> the flesh, the lust of the eyes, and the pride of life--is
> not of the Father, but is of the world.

Variations of these same temptations were used in Eden to ensnare Adam and Eve.

> Gen. 3:6 So when the woman saw the tree *was* good
> for food, that it *was* pleasant to the eyes, and a tree
> desirable to make *one* wise, she took of its fruit, and
> ate. She also gave to her husband with her; and he
> ate.

The same enticements were employed against our Lord in His temptation in the wilderness.

> Mt. 4:3 Now when the tempter came to Him, he
> said, If You are the Son of God, command that these
> stones become bread.

> Mt. 4:5 Then the devil took Him up into the holy
> city, set Him on the pinnacle of the temple,
> Mt. 4:6 And said to Him, If you are the Son of God,
> throw Yourself down: For it is written, He shall give
> His angels charge over you: and in *their* hands they
> shall bear you up, lest you dash your foot against a
> stone.

> Mt. 4:8 Again, the devil took Him up on an
> exceeding high mountain, and showed Him all the
> kingdoms of the world and their glory;
> Mt. 4:9 And he said to Him, All these things I will
> give You if You will fall down and worship me.

Satan will adapt his methods to our situations to entice us into sin. This has been the devil's program for the children of men from the beginning because he knows it is impossible for the love of God to co-exist in our hearts with the love of the world and its pleasures. That is the reason John commanded...

> 1 John 2:15 Do not <u>love the world</u> or the things *that are* in the world. <u>If anyone loves the world, the love of the Father is not in him.</u>

Given the environment of evil in which we live and Satan's relentless assaults, there is an important question we need to ask.

How is it possible to remain rightly related to Jesus when we fall into temptation and sin against God?

John told us we have an Advocate (Greek: *para-cletos*- one called alongside to help) in heaven.

> 1 John 2:1 My little children, these things I write to you, so that you may not sin. And if anyone sins, <u>we have an Advocate with the Father, Jesus Christ the righteous:</u>

According to Thayer's Greek Lexicon, the word translated *advocate* is used of 1) One who pleads another's cause before a judge, hence a lawyer, advocate, or defense attorney; 2) One who pleads another's cause as with an intercessor or mediator; 3) And one called alongside to help, aid, or assist. At this very moment, Jesus is seated at the Father's right hand representing, advocating, and interceding for us.

The One who is our Advocate in heaven is also the propitiation for our sins.

> 1 John 2:2 And He Himself is the propitiation for our sins: and not for ours only, but also for the whole world.

Propitiation (Greek: *hilasmos* - appeasement) means the legal satisfaction for *all* our sins. Jesus' blood shed on Calvary and sprinkled on the mercy seat in the heavenly sanctuary is the once and for all sacrifice for our sins and iniquities. Concerning the coming Messiah, Isaiah prophesied...

> Isa. 53:10 Yet it pleased the LORD to bruise Him; He has put *Him* to grief. When You make His soul an offering for sin, He shall see *His* seed, He shall prolong *His* days, and the pleasure of the LORD shall prosper in His hand.
> Isa. 53:11 He shall see of the labor of His soul, *and* be satisfied. By His knowledge My righteous servant shall justify many, for He shall bear their iniquities.

The writer of Hebrews also declared of Jesus...

> Heb. 10:12 But this Man, after He had offered one sacrifice for sins forever, sat down at the right hand of God,
> Heb. 10:13 From that time waiting till His enemies are made His footstool.
> Heb. 10:14 For by one offering He has perfected forever those who are being sanctified.

Jesus appeased the wrath of God against our sins through His suffering on the cross. The penalty for every sin and iniquity past, present, and future was paid in full when Messiah Jesus died in our place.

> Isa. 53:5 But He *was* wounded for our transgressions, *He was* bruised for our iniquities; the chastisement for our peace *was* upon Him, and by His stripes we are healed.
> Isa. 53:6 All we like sheep have gone astray; we Have turned, every one, to his own way; and the Lord has laid on Him the iniquity of us all.

To be rightly related to God requires not only an advocate and a propitiation for our sins, but a righteousness that He can accept. When we believe in Jesus, we are justified on the basis of faith and we receive the righteousness (i.e. moral perfection) of God Himself.

> Rom. 3:21 But now the righteousness of God apart from the law is revealed, being witnessed by the Law and the Prophets;
> Rom. 3:22 Even the righteousness of God, through faith in Jesus Christ, to all and on all who believe: For there is no difference:

Our sin debt has been paid in full, the righteousness of Jesus has been imputed to us (i.e. reckoned to our account), and we have an advocate in heaven Jesus Christ the Righteous One. Our standing before God is eternally secured by the promise of God Himself.

> John 10:27 My sheep hear My voice, and I know them, and they follow Me:
> John 10:28 And I give them eternal life; and they shall never perish, neither shall anyone snatch them out of My hand.
> John 10:29 My Father, who has given *them* to Me, is greater than all; and no *one* is able to snatch *them* out of My Father's hand.
> John 10:30 I and *My* Father are one.

Although our *standing* with God can never be compromised or endangered, our *fellowship* with God is another matter. A child's behavior reflects on his parents. He may behave in a way that embarrasses them, but he is still the child of his dad and mom. Nothing can change that. Nevertheless, if his behavior is shameful to his parents, it will certainly affect his fellowship with mom and dad. So, how does God provide for this aspect of our relationship with Him? What happens when sin breaks our fellowship with God?

God is light (unqualified purity, utter righteousness, absolute truth) with not even the slightest mixture of darkness (impurity, unrighteousness, or unreality). To maintain our fellowship with Him, we must walk—live our daily lives—in the light. As we walk in the light as God is in the light, we enjoy unhindered fellowship with other believers who likewise walk according to the truth. We also experience continual cleansing in the blood of Jesus.

> 1 John 1:7 But if we walk in the light as He is in the light, <u>we have fellowship with one another,</u> and <u>the blood of Jesus Christ His Son cleanses us from all sin</u>.

To remain in fellowship with God, we cannot hide our disobedience. When we fall into an occasion of sin, we must own it and confess it.

The word translated *confess* is based on two Greek words *homo* (the same) and *logeo* (to say or speak). Hence, *confess* means to say the same thing or agree with what God is saying about our sin. It is to have the mind of Christ about what I have done. If the Spirit of Truth is convicting me of wrongdoing and I say anything else (e.g. "I couldn't help it, It wasn't so bad, Everybody else is doing it, or I don't see anything wrong with it"), I am not agreeing with God. Agreement or oneness is essential for forgiveness and cleansing.

> 1 John 1:9 <u>If we confess</u> our sins, <u>He is faithful and just to forgive</u> us *our* sins <u>and to cleanse</u> us from all unrighteousness.

To ignore, excuse, rationalize, deny, or fail to agree with God about our sin is tantamount to calling God a liar.

> 1 John 1:10 <u>If we say that we have not sinned, we make Him a liar</u>, and His word is not in us.

When we confess our sins, we declare that God is righteous.

After his adultery with Bathsheba, David initially tried to hide his sin. Psalm 32 described a tormented king, refusing to acknowledge his sin. By his silence, he denied his sin and *faulted* God instead of taking responsibility for his behavior.

> Ps. 32:3 <u>When I kept silent</u>, my bones grew old through my groaning all the day long.
> Ps. 32:4 For day and night Your hand was heavy upon me: my vitality was turned into the drought of summer.

However, after being confronted and exposed by the prophet Nathan, the broken and contrite king confessed his transgression. He agreed with God's estimation of his sin and *justified* God.

> Ps. 51:3 For <u>I acknowledge my transgressions</u>: and my sin *is* always before me.
> Ps. 51:4 Against You, You only, <u>have I sinned, and done *this* evil</u> in Your sight—<u>that You may be found just when You speak, *and* blameless when You judge</u>.

God provided all that is necessary for us to be rightly related to Him when He gave us His Son. Jesus is our *Advocate* (i.e. Lawyer, Mediator, and Helper) with the Father, and He ever lives to make intercession for us. Jesus is the *propitiation* (i.e. the legal satisfaction) for all our sins, so we are not subject to divine wrath. Jesus has given us His *righteousness* (i.e. His perfect standing before God), so we have unconditional acceptance with the Father. Moreover, if we yield to temptation in a moment of weakness, all we need to do is step out of the darkness and back into the light by confessing our sin. When we agree with God and repent of our sin, our fellowship is restored. When we have the mind of Christ about our sin, the blood of Jesus Christ cleanses us from all unrighteousness.

How do you deal with sin and iniquity in your life? Do you ignore, excuse, or rationalize wrongdoing? Do you justify wrong thoughts, words, actions, attitudes, or motives? Do you welcome the light of truth into your heart, agree with God, and confess your sin? Are you keeping short accounts with God, or is there a backlog of sin that you have conveniently forgotten?

Rev 12:10

5- OMNISCIENCE OR OBEDIENCE

In John's gospel, we read concerning Jesus' relationship with His Father...

> John 11:41 Then they took away the stone *from the place* where the dead man was lying. <u>And Jesus lifted up *His* eyes and said, Father, I thank You that You have heard Me</u>.
> John 11:42 <u>And I know that You always hear Me</u>, but because of the people who are standing by I said *this*, that they may believe that You sent Me.
> John 11:43 Now when He had said these things, He cried with a loud voice, Lazarus, come forth.
> John 11:44 And he who had died came out, bound hand and foot with grave clothes, and his face was wrapped with a cloth. Jesus said to them, Loose him, and let him go.

Let's begin this chapter by asking what may seem to be a simple question.

How did Jesus know the Father had already heard Him?

Even before He returned to Bethany after getting word from Mary and Martha about their brother's illness, Jesus assured "the twelve" that Lazarus' sickness would not result in death and that He was going to awaken him.

> John 11:4 When Jesus heard that, He said, <u>This sickness is not unto death</u>, but for the glory of God, that the Son of God my be glorified through it.

How could Jesus be so confident of the outcome? Some would say it was because He was deity, and He could do anything God could do because He was God in the flesh. However, let me remind you of what Jesus said about His ministry.

* The Son was powerless of Himself to do anything, so He joined the Father in His activity.

> John 5:19 Then Jesus answered and said to them, Most assuredly, I say to you, <u>The Son can do nothing of Himself</u>, but what He sees the Father do: for whatever He does, the Son also does in like manner.

* The words that He spoke were not of His on design, authority, or initiative but of the Father who was also dwelling in Him and doing the works.

> John 14:10 Do you not believe that I am in the Father, and the Father in Me? <u>The words that I speak to you I speak not of My own authority (of myself): but the Father who dwells in Me does the works.</u>

* His doctrine was not His own but the Father's.

> John 7:16 Jesus answered them and said, <u>My doctrine is not mine, but His who sent Me</u>.

* He spoke those things He had heard from the Father.

> John 8:26 I have many things to say and to judge concerning you, but He who sent Me is true; and <u>I speak to the world those things which I heard from Him</u>.
> John 8:27 They did not understand that He spoke to them of the Father.

* The Father revealed to Him what He was to say.

> John 8:28 Then said Jesus unto them, When you lift up the Son of man, then you will know that I am *He*, and *that* I do nothing of Myself; but as My Father taught Me, I speak these things.

* He did not speak of Himself, but the Father commanded Him what He was to say.

> John 12:49 For I have not spoken on My own *authority* (of myself); but the Father who sent Me gave Me a command, what I should say, and what I should speak.
> John 12:50 And I know that His command is everlasting life: Therefore whatever I speak, just as the Father has told Me, so I speak.

Repeatedly, Jesus testified of His relationship to the Father. He explained that the Father was speaking and working through Him. Jesus was absolutely obedient to and totally dependent on His Father in heaven and did not assert His deity to accomplish His mission. Although He never ceased to be God, He laid aside the prerogatives of deity—the rights and privileges that were exclusively His as God—when He took on human flesh. He did not exercise His omnipresence to be everywhere all the time,

> John 11:20 Now Martha, as soon as she heard that Jesus was coming, went and met Him, but Mary was sitting in the house.
> John 11:21 Now Martha said to Jesus, Lord, if You had been here, my brother would not have died.

…His omnipotence to do all things,

> Mk. 6:4 But Jesus said to them, A prophet is not without honor, except in his own country, among his own relatives, and in his own house.
> Mk. 6:5 Now He could do no mighty work there, except that He laid His hands on a few sick people and healed *them*.

…His omniscience to know all things,

> Mk. 13:32 But of that day and hour no one knows, not even the angels in heaven, nor the Son, but only the Father.

…His independence to do whatever He pleased,

> Rom. 15:2 Let each of us please *his* neighbour for *his* good, leading to edification.
> Rom. 15:3 For even Christ did not please Himself; but as it is written, The reproaches of those who reproached You fell on Me.

…His eternality to never die, etc.

> Lk. 23:46 And when Jesus had cried out with a loud voice, He said, Father, into Your hands I commit My spirit. Having said this, He breathed His last (gave up the spirit).

All that He said and did was as the Son of man relying on His heavenly Father.

Since Jesus always did what was pleasing to the Father, God was continually revealing to His Son what He was doing. Jesus then simply joined the Father in His activity.

> ✗ John 5:19 Then Jesus answered and said to them, Most assuredly, I say to you, The Son can do nothing of Himself, but what He sees the Father do: for whatever He does, the Son also does in like manner.

Like a hand in a glove, God was dwelling in the man, Christ Jesus, teaching Him what to say and supplying the power to do the works.

> John 14:10 Do you not believe that I am in the Father, and the Father in Me? The words that I speak to you I speak not of My own authority (of myself): but the Father who dwells in Me does the works.

In answer to the question posed at the beginning of this chapter, I am suggesting that Jesus knew the Father had heard Him as well as what was going to happen, not because of His *omniscience* but because of His *obedience*. By always obeying the Father, He remained in the Father's love.

> John 15:10 If you keep My commandments, you will abide in My love; just as I have kept my Father's commandments and abide in His love.

The Father expressed His love to the Son by self-revelation, i.e., showing Jesus all that He was doing and then bringing Him into His activity.

> John 5:20 For the Father loves the Son, and shows Him all things that He Himself does: and He will show Him greater works than these, that you may marvel.

Jesus expressed His love to the Father by doing what the Father said, and the Father expressed His love to the Son by continually showing Jesus what He was doing. Jesus simply agreed with God and did whatever the Father was doing.

> John 10:30 I and *My* Father are one.

Consequently, when Jesus prayed at the tomb of Lazarus, He was not throwing rocks in the dark like we often do, hoping to hit something. When He ministered, it was not of His own initiative or resources. When He taught, it was not His doctrine but the Father's. When He worked miracles, it was not by His own strength, ability, or authority. Every day, He listened to the Father and joined Him in what He was doing.

> John 5:17 But Jesus answered them, My Father has been working until now, and I have been working.

Jesus' trust in God and His unconditional obedience allowed Him to know what His Father was doing and brought Him into God's activity.

Much of what passes for "Christian ministry" today is merely human energy and enthusiasm, supported by Madison Avenue business practices. That is why the church is steadily losing ground and so much of our effort yields results that fall far short of the "much fruit" and "fruit that remains" that Jesus promised to those who abide in the vine and rely on Him. Could it be that what is needed to revive our hearts and ignite the church with New Testament power and zeal is a return to the simplicity of the relationship Jesus described in John 15—you and me trusting and obeying Him as He produces the results?

> John 15:5 I am the vine, you *are* the branches: <u>He who abides in Me, and I in him, bears much fruit</u>: for without Me you can do nothing.

Are you identified with Jesus and obedient to Him as He was to the Father? Is He bringing you into His activity and producing much fruit that remains? Are you consciously and continually depending on Him as He depended on His Father?

Through the Bible
Prayer
Circumstances
Through other people
Holy Spirit

6- THE ABUNDANT LIFE

The next question we need to explore is…

What does Jesus' relationship to the Father have to do with you and me?

If you examine what Jesus said about Himself in relation to His Father, you will discover that He described the relationship of believers to Himself in the same terms. In other words, those who have been born again have been placed in a similar relationship with Jesus that He enjoyed with His Father. Notice the following eleven specific parallels:

* Just as Jesus was in the Father and the Father was in Jesus, Jesus is in us and we are in Him.

> John 14:11   Believe Me that I *am* in the Father and the Father in Me: or else believe Me for the sake of the works themselves.

> John 15:4   Abide in Me, and I in you. As the branch cannot bear fruit of itself, unless it abides in the vine; neither can you, unless you abide in Me.

* Just as the Father and Son were always in perfect agreement, sharing fully the attribute of glory known as oneness or unity, Jesus gives to us the same glory—to share oneness with Himself.

> John 10:29 My Father, who has given *them* to Me, is greater than all; and no one is able to snatch *them* out of My Father's hand.
> John 10:30 I and *My* Father are one.

> John 17:22 And the glory which You gave Me I have given them, that they may be one just as We are one:

* Just as the Father loved the Son, Jesus loves us.

> John 15:9 As the Father has loved Me, I also have loved you: abide in My love.

* Just as the Son remained in the Father's love by obedience, we remain in Jesus' love through obedience.

> John 15:10 If you keep My commandments, you will abide in My love, just as I have kept My Father's commandments and abide in His love.

* Just as the Father expressed His love for the Son through self-revelation, Jesus expresses His love for us in the same way.

> John 5:20 For the Father loves the Son, and shows Him all things that He Himself does: and He will show Him greater works than these, that you may marvel.

> John 14:21 He who has My commandments, and keeps them, it is he who loves Me. And he who loves Me will be loved by My Father, and I will love him, and manifest Myself to him.

* Just as the Father sent Jesus, Jesus sends us.

> John 8:42 Jesus said to them, If God were your Father, you would love Me: for I proceeded forth

and came from God; <u>nor have I come of Myself,
but He sent Me</u>.

John 20:21 So Jesus said to them again, Peace to
you! <u>As the Father has sent Me, I also send you</u>.

* Just as Jesus was unable to do anything of Himself and worked
in unison with His Father, we can do nothing if we are not
empowered by and one with Jesus.

John 5:19 Then Jesus answered and said to them,
Most assuredly, I say to you, <u>The Son can do nothing
of Himself,</u> but what He sees the Father do: for
whatever He does, the Son also does in like manner.

John 15:5 I am the vine, you *are* the branches: <u>He
who abides in Me, and I in him</u>, bears much fruit: <u>for
without Me you can do nothing</u>.

* Just as the Son worked the works of His Father, we work the
works of Jesus.

John 9:4 <u>I must work the works of Him who sent
Me</u> while it is day:

John 14:12 Most assuredly, I say to you, <u>he who
believes in Me, the works that I do he will do also</u>;
and greater works than these he will do, because I
go to My Father.

* Just as the Father did His works through the Son, Jesus
has promised to do His works through us.

John 14:10 Do you not believe that I am in the
Father, and the Father in Me? The words that I speak
to you I do not speak on My own authority (of
myself): <u>but the Father who dwells in Me does the
works</u>.

John 14:12 Most assuredly, I say to you, he who
believes in Me, <u>the works that I do he will do also</u>;

and greater works than these he will do, because I go to My Father.

John 14:13 And whatever you ask in My name, that I will do, that the Father may be glorified in the Son.

John 14:14 If you ask anything in My name, I will do it.

Two other parallels that will attain their ultimate fulfillment in the Messianic Kingdom are found in the messages to the churches at Thyatira and Laodicea in Revelation 2 & 3.

* Just as the Father has given the Son authority over the nations, Jesus will give us authority over the nations.

Ps. 2:7 I will declare the decree: the LORD has said to Me, You *are* my Son, Today I have begotten You.

Ps. 2:8 Ask of Me, and I will give You the nations *for* your inheritance, and the ends of the earth *for* Your possession.

Ps. 2:9 You shall break them with a rod of iron; You shall dash them in pieces like a potter's vessel.

Rev. 2:26 And he who overcomes, and keeps My works until the end, to him I will give power over the nations—

Rev. 2:27 He shall rule them with a rod of iron; They shall be dashed to pieces like the potter's vessels—as I also have received from My Father.

* Just as the Son sat down with the Father in His throne, Jesus will grant to us to sit with Him in His throne.

Rev. 3:21 To him who overcomes I will grant to sit with Me on My throne, as I also overcame and sat down with My Father on His throne.

In light of the foregoing evidence, it is clear that salvation is not just about escaping Hell and going to Heaven. It is not merely trusting Jesus as your Savior and trying to do the best you can until you die or Jesus returns. Salvation is much more. It is about

41

enjoying a personal, intimate relationship with Jesus Christ, modeled after His relationship with the Father. It is about believing, obeying, and joining Jesus in what He is doing the way He believed, obeyed, and joined the Father in His activity. It is about you and me being the glove on Jesus' hand. It is about asking and receiving that our joy may be full. It is about doing God's will rather than our own and bringing forth much fruit that remains for His glory.

This relationship is what you and I were made for, and it is the only way anyone can enjoy true meaning and purpose in life. This is the life of joy and victory God desires for every one of His children. It is the life Jesus came to give us.

> John 10:10 The thief does not come, except to steal, and to kill, and to destroy. I have come that they may have life, and that they may have *it* more abundantly.

In his book, *Renewed Day By Day*, A. W. Tozer wrote,

> "If we cooperate with Him *in loving obedience, God will manifest Himself to us,* and that manifestation will be the difference between *a nominal Christian life* and *a life radiant with the light of His face.*"
> (Emphasis added)

Would you describe your relationship with Jesus in terms of *abundant* life? Are you abiding in Jesus, and is He abiding in you? Is Jesus expressing His love to you by self-revelation? Are you remaining in His love by keeping His word? Is Jesus working His works through you?

paradym:

7- THE OTHER COMFORTER

At this juncture, a very important question is in order. Since Jesus has returned to the Father,

How is a personal, intimate relationship with Him possible?

Jesus is no longer physically present, but when He left, He sent the Holy Spirit just as He promised.

The Spirit of God is not merely a force or influence. He is the third person of the Trinity, possessing all the attributes of deity. The Holy Spirit is called God. When Peter confronted Ananias for pretense and deception we read…

> Acts 5:3 But Peter said, Ananias, why has Satan filled your heart to lie to the Holy Spirit and keep back *part* of the price of the land for yourself?
> Acts 5:4 While it remained, was it not your own? And after it was sold, was it not in your own control? Why have you conceived this thing in your heart? You have not lied to men but to God.

The Holy Spirit is synonymous with the presence of God and is therefore omnipresent.

> Ps. 139:7 Where can I go from Your Spirit? Or where can I flee from Your presence?
> Ps. 139:8 If I ascend into heaven, You *are* there; if I make my bed in hell, behold, You *are there*.
> Ps. 139:9 *If* I take the wings of the morning, *and* dwell in the uttermost parts of the sea,
> Ps. 139:10 Even there Your hand shall lead me, and Your right hand shall hold me.

The Spirit of the Lord searches and knows the deep things of God and must be omniscient as well.

> 1 Cor. 2:9 But as it is written: Eye has not seen, nor ear heard, nor have entered into the heart of man the things which God has prepared for those who love Him.
> 1 Cor. 2:10 But God has revealed them to us through His Spirit. For the Spirit searches all things, yes, the deep things of God.
> 1 Cor. 2:11 For what man knows the things of a man except the spirit of the man which is in him? Even so no one knows the things of God except the Spirit of God.

The Holy Spirit was present at the Creation, moving over the surface of the primeval waters. He spoke through the prophets. He beget, empowered, and raised Jesus from the dead. The Spirit of the Lord inspired both Old and New Testament Scriptures. He filled the early church on Pentecost, and continues His work in the world today. Thus, He is called the eternal Spirit.

> Heb. 9:13 For if the blood of bulls and goats and the ashes of a heifer, sprinkling the unclean, sanctifies for the purifying of the flesh,
> Heb. 9:14 How much more shall the blood of Christ, who through the eternal Spirit offered Himself without spot to God, cleanse your conscience from dead works to serve the living God?

The selfsame Holy Spirit was sent by Jesus to be everything to the church that He had been to His disciples.

> John 14:16 And I will pray the Father, and He will give you <u>another Helper (Comforter), that He may abide with you for ever</u>—
> John 14:17 The Spirit of truth, whom the world cannot receive, because it neither sees Him nor knows Him: <u>but you know Him, for He dwells with you, and will be in you.</u>
> John 14:18 I will not leave you orphans; <u>I will come to you.</u>

The Holy Spirit is called *another* (Greek: *allos*) Helper, i.e., not another of a different kind but another of the same kind. Through the person of the Holy Spirit, Jesus comes to us, indwells us, helps and comforts us, and abides with us forever. Moreover, when we receive the Holy Spirit, we also have the Father.

> John 14:23 Jesus answered and said to him, If anyone loves Me, he will keep My word; and My Father will love him, <u>and We will come to him and make Our home with him.</u>

This promise of God's abiding presence was initially fulfilled at Pentecost, but it continues to be fulfilled every time anyone believes and receives Jesus.

Part of the Spirit's work is to teach, and bring the things of Christ to our remembrance. That is how the disciples were able to write the Scriptures.

> John 14:26 But the Helper (Comforter), the Holy Spirit, whom the Father will send in My name, <u>He will teach you all things, and bring to your remembrance all things that I said to you.</u>

The Holy Spirit is called the Spirit of grace because He supplies both the desire and power to do God's will. He awakens and leads men to repentance. In the days just before Christ's return, He will give Israel a heart to seek the Lord, and they will accept Jesus as their long awaited Messiah.

> Zech. 12:10 And I will pour on the house of David and on the inhabitants of Jerusalem <u>the Spirit of</u>

45

grace and supplication; then they will look on Me
whom they pierced. Yes, they will mourn for Him
as one mourns for *his* only *son,* and grieve for Him
as one grieves for a firstborn.

Through the person of the Holy Spirit, Jesus is present in His
Church authorizing, revealing, directing, and enabling kingdom
advance just as if He was physically present.

Mt. 28:18 And Jesus came and spoke to them,
saying, All authority has been given to Me in heaven
and on earth.
Mt. 28:19 Go therefore and make disciples of all the
nations, baptizing them in the name of the Father
and of the Son and of the Holy Spirit,
Mt. 28:20 Teaching them to observe all things that I
have commanded you; and, lo, I am with you always,
even to the end of the age. Amen.

The Spirit of God does not call attention to Himself, but bears
witness to Jesus.

John 15:26 But when the Helper (Comforter) comes,
whom I shall send to you from the Father, the Spirit
of truth, who proceeds from the Father, He will
testify of Me.

As Jesus was under the authority of the Father, the Holy Spirit is
submissive to the Son, not speaking of Himself, but speaking only
what He hears from Jesus.

John 16:13 However, when He, the Spirit of truth,
has come, He will guide you into all truth; for He
will not speak on His on authority (of himself); but
whatever He hears He will speak; and He will tell
you things to come.

Ultimately, the Holy Spirit desires to express His nature and
life—the very life of Jesus—in our physical bodies. As we yield to
His filling (i.e. control), He transforms us and conforms us to the
likeness of Christ.

> 2 Cor. 4:7 But <u>we have this treasure in earthen vessels</u>, that the excellence of the power may be of God and not of us.
> 2 Cor. 4:8 *We are* hard-pressed on every side, yet not crushed; *we are* perplexed, but not in despair;
> 2 Cor. 4:9 Persecuted, but not forsaken; struck down, but not destroyed—
> 2 Cor. 4:10 Always carrying about in the body the dying of the Lord Jesus, <u>that the life of Jesus also may be manifested in our body</u>.

Through the Holy Spirit, Jesus is present in His church. All the power needed to do whatever Jesus commanded is available and supplied by His Spirit.

> Luke 24:49   Behold, <u>I send the promise of My Father upon you</u>; but tarry in the city of Jerusalem until <u>you are endued with power from on high</u>.

To fully experience the life of Christ in our mortal bodies, we must be filled with the presence of Jesus, i.e., fully surrendered to and controlled by the Holy Spirit.

In the devotional classic, *My Utmost For His Highest*, Oswald Chambers affirmed,

> April 12- *Eternal life was the life that Jesus Christ exhibited* on the human plane, and it is *the same life* not a copy of it, *which is manifested in our mortal flesh when we are born of God…The life that was in Jesus becomes ours because of His Cross*, once we make the decision to be identified with Him…*Even the weakest saint can experience the power of the deity of the Son of God*, when he is willing to "let go." But any effort to "hang on" to the least bit of our own power will only diminish *the life of Jesus in us*. We have to keep letting go, and slowly, but surely, *the great full life of God* will invade us in every part, and people will take notice that we have been with Jesus." (Emphasis added)

Holy Spirit filling is not a matter of quantity—you are not 25%, 50%, 75%, or 100% filled with the Spirit. Spirit filling is a matter of control. As Dr. Adrian Rogers would say, "It is not how much of the Holy Spirit you have, but how much the Holy Spirit has of you." To the degree that you and I are surrendered and obedient to Jesus, to that same degree we are filled with His presence and empowered to do His works.

Have you failed to honor the person and work of the Holy Spirit in your life? Is the Holy Spirit teaching and revealing the things of Christ to you? Is He transforming and conforming you to the likeness of Jesus? Is the life of the Son of God being manifested increasingly in your life?

Old Covenant   New Covenant
    "LAW"   "Grace"

8- A NEW PARADIGM

The next question I would like for us to consider is…

How does Christ's redemption impact you and me?

Jesus' redemption, exaltation to the Father's right hand, and the coming of the Holy Spirit to indwell believers has made possible a new paradigm. The new birth places us in the same relationship with Jesus that He enjoyed with the Father. Now, we are to believe on Jesus and continue His work, controlled and empowered by His Spirit.

Before He returned to the Father, Jesus lived life as a perfect man, trusting perfectly in His heavenly Father. As we have seen, He laid aside the prerogatives of deity to live among us as the Son of man. Though He did not cease to be God, He chose not to exercise His rights and privileges as God during His incarnation. As a man, He fully experienced the joys and sorrows of life, and then willingly submitted to the shame and humiliation of death by crucifixion.

> Heb. 5:8 Though He was a Son, yet learned He obedience by the things which He suffered.

49

As He faced the cross, Jesus told "the twelve" a new day was about to dawn when all their questions would be answered and they would learn to pray and approach God in a new way. Significant changes were about to occur in the way they related to Jesus and the Father, and the way Jesus and the Father would relate to them. There would be a change in Jesus' *location*—I am going to my Father.

> John 16:16 A little while, and you will not see Me;
> and again a little while, and you will see Me, <u>because</u>
> <u>I go to the Father.</u>

There was to be a change in the disciples' *privilege*—they would ask and receive in Jesus' name.

> John 16:23 And in that day you will ask Me nothing.
> <u>Most assuredly, I say to you, whatever you ask the</u>
> <u>Father in My name, He will give you.</u>
> John 16:24 <u>Until now you have asked nothing in My</u>
> <u>Name. Ask, and you will receive, that your joy may</u>
> <u>be full.</u>

There would be a change in Jesus' *practice*—no longer would it be necessary for Jesus to pray the Father for them because they would be able to ask for themselves.

> John 16:26 <u>In that day you will ask in My name,</u>
> and <u>I do not say to you that I shall pray the Father for</u>
> <u>you;</u>

There would be a change in the disciples' *perception*—they would come to know the love and acceptance of the Father as Jesus did.

> John 16:27 <u>For the Father Himself loves you,</u>
> because you have loved Me, and have believed that
> I came forth from God.

> John 20:17 Jesus said to her, Do not cling to Me, for
> I have not yet ascended to My Father; but go to My
> brethren and say to them, <u>I am ascending to My</u>
> <u>Father and your Father, and *to* My God, and your</u>
> <u>God.</u>

During Jesus' ministry His relationship with the disciples was different. He prayed to the Father, and He taught them to pray to the Father. They did not pray to Jesus as God, but He prayed to the Father on their behalf. As they accompanied Him, He did the works of God.

> John 17:9 <u>I pray for them</u>. I do not pray for the world but <u>for those whom You have given me</u>, for they are Yours.
>
> John 17:11 Now I am no longer in the world, but these are in the world, and I come to You. Holy Father, <u>keep through Your name those whom You have given Me, that they may be one as We</u> *are*.

In consequence of Jesus' return to the Father, the disciples were no longer to be observers and helpers, but *co-workers* with Jesus.

> John 14:12 Most assuredly, I say to you, <u>he who believes in Me, the works that I do he will do also; and greater *works* than these he will do</u>...

What fundamental difference made possible this new relationship of asking and receiving in Jesus' name and joining Him in his activity?

> John 14:12 ...<u>because I go to My Father</u>.

Jesus' death and subsequent resurrection and exaltation to the right hand of God meant His work was complete, sufficient, and effectual. Now, He has taken up the prerogatives of deity that He laid aside in the incarnation. As God, He hears and answers prayer, but it must be offered to the Father in His name. Twice in back-to-back promises, Jesus pledged to do whatever we ask *in His name*.

> John 14:13 And whatever you ask in My name, <u>that I will do</u>, that the Father may be glorified in the Son.
> John 14:14 If ye shall ask any thing in My name, <u>I will do *it*</u>.

Asking and receiving are essential to working Jesus' works and continuing His mission. Moreover, they are essential to fullness of joy in this new relationship.

> John 16:22 Therefore you now have sorrow; but I will see you again and your heart will rejoice, and your joy no one will take from you.
> John 16:23 And in that day you will ask Me nothing. Most assuredly, I say to you, whatever you ask the Father in My name, He will give you.
> John 16:24 Until now you have asked nothing in My Name. Ask, and you will receive, that your joy may be full.

What does it mean to ask in Jesus' name? If we preface or end our prayer with the words, "in Jesus' name," are we meeting the requirement? Does being sincere in our faith and speaking these words with volume and enthusiasm mean God must give us what we ask?

Clearly, there is more to asking in Jesus' name than reciting a formula at the end of our prayer. Think about it—why would Jesus give us His name as a cosmic credit card with no limits? So we can satisfy our heart's desire? So we can be healthy wealthy, and wise and enjoy our "best life now" as some teach? Is prayer just about our needs and what we want, or is it about something bigger, more important, and enduring?

Jesus said, "To whom much is given much is required." He has given us much when He gave us His name and authority to use it, and He expects much from us. In fact, Jesus expects no less from us than His Father expected of Him. Moreover, what He requires He supplies, and what He commands He enables.

As the exalted Man, Jesus has lifted us into the very presence of God where *in Christ* we have been graciously endowed with all the privileges of Son-ship. We are blessed with all spiritual blessings in heavenly places, chosen before the foundation of the world, holy and without blame before Him in love, predestinated unto the adoption of children, accepted in the Beloved, and redeemed through His blood. We are heirs of God, forgiven of all our sins, sealed with the Holy Spirit of promise, greatly loved, made alive together with Christ, saved by grace, raised up together with Him, seated with Christ in heavenly places, made nigh by the blood, reconciled to God by the cross, and given access by one Spirit unto the Father. We are fellow-citizens with the saints, of the household of God, a purchased possession, built upon the foundation of the apostles and prophets, fitted together, growing into a holy temple in the Lord, and a dwelling place of God through the Spirit. (See Eph. 1 & 2).

All that Jesus did is now credited to us by virtue of our union with Him. We are crucified with Christ and dead with Him from the basic principles of the world, buried with Him in baptism, quickened together with Him by the Spirit, risen with Him through faith in the working of God, seated together with Christ at the Father's right hand, and hidden with Christ in God (See Col. 2 & 3). No wonder John, the beloved apostle, wrote…

> 1 John 3:1 <u>Behold, what manner of love the Father has bestowed on us, that we should be called children of God</u>! Therefore the world does not know us, because it did not know Him.

No wonder Paul prayed that we might understand the glorious destiny that is ours as a result of Christ's redemption.

> Eph. 1:15 Therefore I also, after I heard of your faith in the Lord Jesus and love for all the saints,
> Eph. 1:16 Do not cease to give thanks for you, making mention of you in my prayers:
> Eph. 1:17 That the God of our Lord Jesus Christ, the Father of glory, <u>may give to you the spirit of wisdom and revelation in the knowledge of Him</u>,
> Eph. 1:18 <u>The eyes of your understanding being enlightened; that you may know what is the hope of His calling</u>, and what are <u>the riches of the glory of His inheritance in the saints</u>,
> Eph. 1:19 And what *is* <u>the exceeding greatness of</u>

His power toward us who believe, according to the
working of His mighty power...

Manley Beasley once said that Jesus Christ lived life the way
God intended every man to live it. I believe the Scriptural
evidence is overwhelming. Christ's life is our life, Christ's victory
is our victory, Christ's authority is our authority, Christ's mission
is our mission, and Christ's destiny is our destiny.

Jesus shares with us all the perfections of His humanity—His
love, joy, peace, patience, gentleness, goodness, faith, meekness,
and self-control. We have the standing of Christ, the mind of
Christ, and the Spirit of Christ. We abide in the love of Christ, we
are members of Christ, we are empowered by Christ, we work the
works of Christ, and we share in the sufferings of Christ. We are
made partakers of Christ, we are filled with the fullness of Christ,
we remain in the grace of Christ, and we are heirs together with
Christ.

The new paradigm made possible by Jesus' redemption,
exaltation, and the coming of the Holy Spirit means we have been
placed in the same relationship with Jesus that He enjoyed with the
Father. Now, washed from our sins by His blood, imputed with
His righteousness, vested with His authority, indwelled by His
presence and controlled by His Spirit, it is possible for us to
continue His mission.

Are you experiencing an increasing joy as you ask and receive
in Jesus' name? Are your prayers about you and what you want or
about Jesus and what He wants? Do you know who you are in
Christ?

9- ASKING AND RECEIVING

A widespread misunderstanding among many Christians is the view that Jesus' prayer promises are *isolated* or *unconditional* promises, rather than assurances in the context of His other teaching. For example, consider the following dual promises.

> John 14:13 <u>And whatever you ask in My name, that I will do,</u> that the Father may be glorified in the Son.
> John 14:14 <u>If ye shall ask any thing in My name, I will do *it*.</u>

Both promises are given in the context of doing Jesus' works as the preceding verse makes clear.

> John 14:12 Most assuredly, I say to you, <u>He who believes in Me, the works that I do he will do also;</u> and <u>greater works than these he will do</u> because I go to My Father.

Consider the following promises:

> John 15:7 If you abide in Me, and My words abide in you, <u>you will ask what you desire, and it shall be done for you.</u>

John 15:16 You did not choose Me, but I chose you
and appointed you that you should go and bear fruit,
and *that* your fruit should remain, that whatever you
ask the Father in My name, He may give you.

These guarantees are given in the context of abiding in Jesus (the condition for asking and receiving) and bringing forth much fruit (the goal and motivation of our requests). Sadly, as a consequence of our failure to see prayer as a means of obtaining the resources needed for continuing our Lord's mission, much of our praying is often misguided and unfruitful. As James wrote,

James 4:3 You ask and do not receive, because you
ask amiss, that you may spend *it* on your pleasures.

At this juncture, it would be helpful to explore the question…

How can we obtain the resources needed to do the works of Jesus?

If we are going to obey Jesus and fulfill the Great Commission, we must have access to the resources Jesus had—we need to be able to draw upon God's unlimited riches. What did Paul write to the Philippians?

Phil. 4:19 And my God shall supply all your need
according to His riches in glory by Christ Jesus.

The Philippian believers had opened their hearts and shared their means repeatedly with Paul, enabling him to do the work of ministry. In light of their faithful support, God promised to supply their needs. Similarly, the Lord will meet our needs when we are committed to bearing much fruit for His glory.

John 15:7 If ye abide in Me, and My words abide
in you, you will ask what you desire, and it shall be
done for you.
John 15:8 By this My Father is glorified, that you
bear much fruit; so you will be My disciples.

Further evidence that the privilege of asking and receiving cannot be divorced from our responsibility to be about the Father's business is found in John 15. In verse 16, there are two purpose clauses introduced by the word *that* (Greek: *hina*).

> John 15:16 You did not choose Me, but I chose you and appointed you that (*hina*) you should go and bear fruit, and *that* your fruit should remain, that (hina) whatever you ask the Father in My name He may give you.

Commenting on the second of the two purpose clauses in the preceding verse (*that whatever you ask...He may give you*), Henry Alford wrote in his critical commentary on the Greek New Testament,

> "This *hina* (in order that) is parallel with the former one, not the result of it; the two, the bringing forth of fruit and the obtaining answer to prayer, being coordinate with each other; but the bearing of fruit to God's glory is of these the greater, being the result and aim of the other" (pg. 861).

In other words, Jesus chose and ordained us *in order that we could go and bear fruit that remains.* He also chose and ordained us *in order that we could ask and receive.* Our responsibility to bear fruit and our privilege to ask and receive are both ordained and inseparable. The one facilitates the other. The asking and receiving in Jesus' name leads to the production of fruit that remains.

Jesus also made it clear that our mission is to believe on Him and continue His mission.

> Mt. 28:19 Go therefore and make disciples of all the nations, baptizing them in the name of the Father and of the Son and of the Holy Spirit,
> Mt. 28:20 Teaching them to observe all things that I have commanded you; and lo, I am with you always, *even* to the end of the age. Amen.

As the resurrected, ascended Lord possessing all authority in heaven and earth, Jesus promised to do whatever we ask in His name as we believe on Him and do His works.

> John 14:12 Most assuredly, I say to you, <u>he who believes in Me, the works that I do he will do also; and greater *works* than these he will do</u>; because I go to My Father.
> John 14:13 And <u>whatever you ask in My name, that I will do,</u> that the Father may be glorified in the Son.
> John 14:14 <u>If you ask any thing in My name, I will do *it*</u>.

Far from being a blank check for Christians to use or abuse as we please, the privilege of asking and receiving in Jesus' name is reserved for those who know Jesus, those who are abiding in Jesus, and those who are carrying out His agenda.

All that Jesus said and did—His works, His preaching, His prayers—all flowed out of His relationship with the Father. What the Father was saying to Him and showing Him determined His asking. He did not have a separate agenda, just the Father's agenda. Similarly, all we do, especially our praying, must flow out of our relationship with the risen exalted Lord Jesus. What is Jesus saying to you, what is He showing you, what is He doing? What is His will for your life, your family, your career, your church, etc.? We cannot join Jesus in our praying if we have our own agenda.

> 1 John 5:14 Now this is the confidence that we have in Him, that <u>if we ask anything according to His will, He hears us</u>.
> 1 John 5:15 And if we know that He hears us, whatever we ask, we know that we have the petitions that we have asked of Him.

Prayer is not so much about us as it is about God. Jesus taught us that prayer is about hallowing God's name, bringing His kingdom, and doing His will on earth as it is being done in heaven. Yes, it also involves securing our daily bread, forgiveness for our trespasses, and protection from the evil one, but only as those things contribute to the realization of His kingdom, power, and glory. God doesn't give us food just to satisfy our hunger, but to strengthen us to serve Him. He doesn't forgive us just so we can sleep at night with a clear conscience, but so we can be rightly related to Him and help others experience His forgiveness. He does not protect us from the evil one so we can live untroubled, carefree lives, but so we can accomplish His purposes in this world.

Jesus could not be more clear. The privilege of asking and receiving is reserved for those who are living in the relationship He described in John 15.

> John 15:5 I am the vine, you *are* the branches. He who abides in Me, and I in him, bears much fruit; for without Me you can do nothing.
>
> John 15:7 If you abide in Me, and My words abide in you, you will ask what you desire, and it shall be done for you.

Abiding in Jesus and bearing much fruit is what it means to be a Christian, a disciple of Jesus Christ. It is not trying to be a good person and keeping a set of rules learned from childhood. It is not attending church once or twice a week and doing whatever we please the rest of the time. It is not serving in some capacity in the church and giving our money to help pay the bills and keep the doors open. Rather, it is living in daily, vital relationship with Jesus, allowing Him to live and express His life through us.

Are you abiding in the true Vine and bringing forth much fruit? Is what you desire the will of God, and is Jesus doing whatever you ask? Are your prayers informed by what Jesus is saying and doing or merely a recitation of your personal wish list? In your praying, are you focused upon kingdom advance and the glory of God or your own agenda?

10- PRAYER IN JESUS' NAME

For many years, I thought praying in Jesus' name meant ending my prayer with the words *in Jesus' name I pray, Amen.* Although my requests were usually selfish, still I thought if I said the words—*in Jesus' name*—God would hear my prayer. After all, He promised, right?

I believe many Christians view prayer in Jesus' name as nothing more than attaching a formula to our laundry list of requests, thinking that somehow just the mention of His name will open Heaven's treasuries. However, what if we pray for something we know is not God's will for our lives? Will the Lord do what we say just because we recite the magic words? Suppose I pray, "Lord, give me my neighbor's wife, and I ask in Jesus' name." Is God obligated to give me what I ask just because I spoke the words "in Jesus' name?" No honest Christian believes that because it is opposed to the will of God as expressed in the word of God. It is at odds with the nature of God. Indeed, it is the exact opposite of praying in Jesus' name because He was all about the will of God and the glory of God.

Well, what about praying, "God, get me out of debt, make me a success, take away my arthritis, restore my failing eyesight, heal my emphysema, give me a bigger church, a better job, a fatter bank account, a happy family, and do it *in Jesus' name?*" These petitions are not necessarily opposed to the will, word, or nature of God, so is He obligated to grant my requests just because I spoke the words "in Jesus' name?" Of course not.

For a few moments let's explore the question…

What does it mean to pray in Jesus' name?

In the Old Testament we learn…
- The Levites ministered in the name of the Lord.
- The prophets spoke in the name of the Lord.
- David fought Goliath in the name of the Lord.
- Jonathan and David swore oaths to each other in the name of the Lord.
- Elijah built an altar on Mt. Carmel in the name of the Lord.
- Elisha cursed some children in the name of the Lord, and they were killed by a bear.
- Israel was commanded to trust in the name of the Lord.
- The Scriptures promised Messiah would come in the name of the Lord.

In the New Testament…
- We receive a child in Jesus' name.
- We gather in Jesus' name.
- We are to cast out devils and do miracles in Jesus' name.
- We give a cup of water in Jesus' name.
- We are warned about false prophets who would deceive many in Jesus' name.
- The Father sent the Spirit in Jesus' name.
- We trust in Jesus' name.
- We are to preach repentance and remission of sins in Jesus' name.
- We are to believe, baptize, and teach in His name.
- We are washed, sanctified, and justified in the name of Jesus.
- We are to pray over the sick anointing them with oil in the name of Jesus.
- We are told to ask and receive in Jesus' name.

As you can see, the concept of acting in someone's name was common in both testaments, but what does the expression mean? A survey of the Scriptures will show the basic idea is *for, because of, on behalf of, acting as an agent, substitute, or proxy of another.* Generally speaking, we may also assume that being sent in one's name would imply *agreement* and *faithfulness.* If you were dealing with weighty matters, you would never send someone to act on your behalf who was not in full agreement with you and completely trustworthy. Some other ideas we can infer would be *authorization, obedience,* and *identification* with one's methodology, wishes, and plans. In addition, we may assume that the *sendee* would be as much like the *sender* as possible; the person sent in the name of another would embody the character of the person who sent him.

In the book of Matthew there is a passage that sheds additional light on this topic.

> Mt. 21:8 And a very great multitude spread their clothes on the road; others cut down branches from the trees, and spread *them* on the road.
> Mt. 21:9 Then the multitudes who went before and those who followed cried out, saying: Hosanna to the Son of David! Blessed *is* He who comes in the name of the LORD! Hosanna in the highest!

The cry of the people in verse 9 was a Messianic greeting taken from Psalm 118. They were proclaiming Jesus as Messiah using a blessing sung at Passover and very familiar to every Jew.

> Ps. 118:26 Blessed *is* he who comes in the name of the LORD! We have blessed you from the house of the LORD.

Jesus also applied these words to Himself in Matthew 23 when He denounced the hypocrisy of the scribes and Pharisees and declared to the multitudes…

> Mt. 23:39 For I say to you, you shall see Me no more till you say, Blessed *is* He who comes in the name of the Lord.

Jesus is the key by which all Scripture is to be interpreted, so if we want to understand a verse, a doctrine, or a Biblical principle, we must understand it in the light of Jesus Christ. Therefore, what did it mean for Jesus to come "in the name of the Lord?" Following is a list of seven criteria implicit in this phrase.

* Jesus came as *God's Son*.

> Mt. 3:16 When He had been baptized, Jesus came up immediately from the water; and behold, the heavens were opened to Him, and He saw the Spirit of God descending like a dove and alighting upon Him.
> Mt. 3:17 And suddenly a voice came from heaven, saying, This is My beloved Son, in whom I am well pleased.

Jesus was *related* to God. He was an obedient Son, the only begotten of the Father.

* He came in *God's way*.

> Isa. 55:8 For My thoughts are not your thoughts, nor are your ways My Ways, says the LORD.

Jesus came in weakness relying on God's strength, in humility instead of pride, in obscurity rather than fame, in poverty as opposed to wealth. He had no beauty that we would desire Him. He lived a life of self-denial versus self-indulgence, serving rather than being served, and willingly lost His life that He might save it.

* Jesus came according to *God's will*.

> Gal. 1:4 Who gave Himself for our sins, that He might deliver us from this present evil age, according to the will of our God and Father:

His death was the will of God, and He always did those things that pleased the Father.

* Jesus came in *God's time*.

> Gal. 4:4 But <u>when the fullness of the time had come,</u>
> <u>God sent forth His Son</u>, born of a woman, born under
> the law,
> Gal. 4:5 To redeem those who were under the law,
> that we might receive the adoption as sons.

He was not early or late but right on time, according to God's schedule.

* Jesus came as *God's agent*.

> John 5:43 <u>I have come in My Father's name</u>, and you
> do not receive Me; if another comes in his own name,
> him you will receive.

Jesus was acting in God's stead. He was anointed and empowered by the Holy Spirit, sent by the Father, and authorized to speak His words and do His works.

* Jesus came in and for *God's glory*.

> John 1:14 And the Word became flesh and dwelt
> among us, <u>and we beheld His glory, the glory as of</u>
> <u>the only begotten of the Father,</u> full of grace and truth.

His life was a reflection of the glory of God. His aim and desire was the glory of His Father.

* Jesus came for *God's purpose*.

> Mt. 20:28 Just as the Son of man did not come to be
> served, but to serve, and <u>to give His life a ransom for</u>
> <u>many</u>.

Jesus coming accomplished many things, but the primary purpose was redemption. He came to shed His blood and buy back the human race from the bondage of sin and death.

Jesus said, "As the Father has sent Me, I also send you." He came in His Father's name, and He sends us in His name. Consequently, we can infer the following:

- Since He was related to the Father as the only begotten Son, we must have a personal relationship with Him.
- Since He came in God's way, He expects us to walk in weakness, humility, obscurity, poverty, self-denial, serving and willingly laying down our lives for His glory.
- Since He came to do the will of God, He expects us to always do His will.
- Since He came according to God's time, He expects us to operate on His schedule.
- Since He came as God's agent, He expects us to act as His agents—sent, anointed, empowered by His Spirit, with authority to work His works and speak His words.
- Since He was all about the glory of His Father, He expects us to reflect and seek His glory at all times and in all situations.
- Since He came for the purpose of redemption, He expects us to live on the basis of redemption, trusting His finished work and bringing the lost to Him.

The previous 7 criteria describe what it meant for Jesus to come in the name of the Lord, and they also teach us what it means to pray in the name of the Lord (Jesus). Prayer in Jesus' name means asking as God's child rightly related to the Father and the Son.

> Mt. 6:9 In this manner, therefore, pray: Our Father in heaven, Hallowed be Your name.

To be rightly related to God does not mean we never sin.

> 1 John 1:8 If we say that we have no sin, we deceive ourselves, and the truth is not in us.

However, to remain in fellowship with the Father and exercise the privilege of asking and receiving in Jesus' name, we must confess and not cover our sin.

Ps. 66:18 If I regard iniquity in my heart, <u>the Lord will not hear.</u>

1 John 1:9 <u>If we confess our sins,</u> He is faithful and just to forgive us *our* sins and to cleanse us from all unrighteousness.

* I pray in Jesus' name when I am God's child and my life is square with Him.

Prayer in Jesus' name means asking in harmony with God's ways. It is asking in weakness depending on God's strength, asking humbly rather than proudly demanding, not seeking the praise of man but praying in secret and trusting the Father to reward us openly. It is asking in poverty not seeking to use prayer to enrich ourselves, in self-denial not self-indulgence, as a servant seeking the good of others, and not seeking to save our lives, but to lose them for the sake of the gospel.

* I pray in Jesus' name when my prayer is in harmony with God's ways.

Prayer in Jesus' name means asking according to God's will. Jesus taught us to pray "Your kingdom come, Your will be done on earth as it is in heaven." We must discover and pray for the will of God as revealed in Scripture.

1 John 5:14 Now this is the confidence that we have in Him, that <u>if we ask any thing according to His will, He hears us</u>:

Priorities we should pray for daily are revival among God's people, awakening among the lost, harvest laborers, the advance of the gospel throughout the world, Israel's restoration and national conversion, the peace of Jerusalem, and the soon return of Christ.

Tragically, too many Christians have not been taught to pray biblically. They have never experienced the joy and excitement of availing prayer as seen in the book of Acts, and they have little appetite for intercessory prayer. In many of our churches, midweek prayer meetings have devolved into a recital of the needs and names of the sick followed by a blanket prayer covering everyone. Ultimate kingdom priorities are displaced by the immediate concerns of the infirm. As my dear friend and Methodist lay-pastor, Jim Roper, would say, "We pray for Uncle Joe's toe, Aunt Lucy's liver, and cousin Bob's job." In fact, we often spend more time talking about needs than actually praying for the needy, and the pressing concerns of the lost are ignored. In a growing number of churches, prayer meeting has been replaced by Bible Study or discontinued entirely.

* I pray in Jesus' name when I ask according to the will of God.

Prayer in Jesus' name means asking in God's time. Prayer has a time component; it is time sensitive. Reflecting on his need of forgiveness, David wrote...

> Ps. 32:6 For this cause everyone who is godly shall pray to You <u>in a time when You may be found</u>; surely in a flood of great waters they shall not come near him.

Throughout Scripture, we are reminded of the importance of the timing of prayer.

> Isa. 55:6 Seek the LORD <u>while He may be found</u>, call upon Him <u>while He is near</u>:

Concerning the end of life, David prayed...

> Ps. 39:13 Remove your gaze from me, that I may regain strength, <u>before I go away and am no more</u>.

Concerning salvation...

> 2 Cor. 6:2 For He says: In an acceptable time I have heard you, and <u>in the day of salvation I have helped you.</u> Behold, <u>now *is* the accepted time</u>; behold, <u>now *is* the day of salvation</u>.

* I pray in Jesus' name when I ask according to God's schedule.

Prayer in Jesus' name means asking as His agent. To act as His agent, we must be able to utilize His authority. However, to exercise authority, we must be under authority. We must be walking in obedience to our Master. Whether bearing witness to Jesus, making disciples, leading a soul to Christ, wrestling with principalities and powers, casting out demons, healing a disease, or claiming a promise from Scripture—if we are obeying Jesus and not acting on our own initiative, we have His authority to do His will. Empowered by the Holy Spirit, we are sent with authority to work the works of Jesus and speak the words of Jesus.

* I pray in Jesus' name when I ask as His agent acting with His authority.

Prayer in Jesus' name means asking for God's glory. Jesus taught us to pray, "Hallowed be Your name" and "Yours is the kingdom and the power and the glory forever." Somehow, we have lost sight of the reason for everything—the creation of the world, the redemption of man, and the consummation of all things when Christ shall deliver up the kingdom to His Father. God created us, chose us, blessed us, predestinated us, purchased us, forgave us, accepted us, and sealed us all to the praise of *His glory*! And God will bring this old world to an end and make every knee bow and tongue confess that Jesus is Lord to His eternal glory. Prayer is not just for our sake; it brings glory to God.

* I pray in Jesus' name when my aim is the glory of God.

Prayer in Jesus' name means asking on the basis of redemption. At the cross, Jesus blotted out our sins and totally defeated Satan and his minions. At the cross, Jesus reconciled to God all things in heaven and earth. We do not fight *for* victory we fight *from* victory. Redemption is an accomplished fact! Moreover, God does not hear us because of our virtue, our good deeds, or because we dot all the i's and cross all the t's. He does not hear us for our much speaking, or even because we pray in faith, pray earnestly, and pray with perseverance. God hears us on the basis of redemption—the reconciliation of all things to the Father through the atoning work of the Son.

* I pray in Jesus' name when I ask on the basis of redemption.

In summary, simply tacking the phrase *in Jesus' name* on the end of your prayer does not make it a prayer in Jesus' name. Prayer in Jesus' name means asking as God's child, asking in harmony with God's ways, asking according to God's will, asking in God's time, asking as God's agent, asking for the glory of God, and asking on the basis of redemption.

Conversely, I do not pray in Jesus' name if I am not rightly related to Him, when my prayer is not in harmony with God's ways, when I do not ask for the will of God, when I do not ask according to God's schedule, when I do not ask in His authority, when my aim is not the glory of God, and when I do not ask on the basis of redemption.

Prayer in Jesus' name is hard, but it is the hardest work you will ever love. It requires thought, practice, study of God's Word, discernment, listening to Jesus, self-examination, and faith. Nevertheless, if you are willing, Jesus will teach you how to pray just as He did His disciples.

When you pray, do you see yourself as Jesus' agent acting on His behalf? Are you in agreement with Jesus, under His authority and identified with His purposes? Are you praying in Jesus' name or just tacking His name on to your requests?

11- JOINING JESUS

Given what we have learned about the way Jesus relates to us, we need to explore the question...

How do we discern where Jesus is working and join Him?

As Henry Blackaby pointed out in his excellent work entitled *Experiencing God*, the Lord is always at work; He is at work all around us. However, we may not recognize His activity at first, so how do we join Him? No matter where we are or what we are doing, if we want to join Jesus in what He is doing, we must obey. *Obedience is what brings us into the activity of God.*

We experience the mighty work of regeneration when we *obey* God's command to repent and believe the gospel.

> Acts 17:30 Truly, these times of ignorance God overlooked, <u>but now (He) commands all men everywhere to repent</u>:

God's ongoing work of sanctification occurs as we believe and *obey* the Word of God. Jesus prayed for us...

> John 17:17 <u>Sanctify them by Your truth</u>. Your word is truth.

The disciples joined Jesus in His activity as they followed Him and *obeyed* His commandments, and it is no different for us. Normally, we prefer to understand first and then decide if we want to participate. However, God's way is to obey first, and then to understand.

> John 7:16 Jesus answered them and said, My doctrine is not Mine, but His who sent Me.
> John 7:17 If anyone wills (desires) to do His will, he shall know concerning the doctrine, whether it is from God or *whether* I speak on my own authority (of myself).

Keeping Jesus' commandments is the prerequisite to knowing what He is doing and where He is working. Obedience is the way we express our love to Him, and He expresses His love to us by disclosing Himself and what He is doing.

> John 14:21 He who has My commandments, and keeps them, it is he who loves Me. And he who loves Me will be loved by My Father, and I will love him, and manifest Myself to him.

Jesus lives in every believer, and He desires to express His life through us. He doesn't want to help us do something for Him. He wants you and me to let Him use our members (eyes, ears, mouth, hands, feet, etc.) for His righteous purposes.

> Rom. 6:13 And do not present your members as instruments of unrighteousness to sin, but present yourselves to God as being alive from the dead, and your members *as* instruments of righteousness to God.

As we decrease, He will increase. As we die to self, He will more and more live His life through us. Jesus will inhabit, possess, and abide in us, and our bodies will be His temple.

Practically speaking, how do we join Jesus in His activity? Whether you are at work, play, shopping, worshipping, visiting with friends, driving down the road, relaxing at home—it does not matter. Do not be so consumed, distracted, or preoccupied by your immediate circumstances and concerns that you miss the opportunity to join Jesus in what He is doing. Cultivate the habit of watching for His activity and listening for His voice.

> John 10:27 <u>My sheep hear My voice</u>, and I know them, and they follow Me:

Ask Jesus, "What are you doing and what do you want me to do? He is in you in the person of the Holy Spirit, so surrender to His control. Let Him speak with your mouth, use your hands to serve, your feet to go where He wants to go, your eyes to see the harvest, your ears to hear the cries of those who are perishing, and your mind to think God's thoughts. Let Jesus hunger and thirst for righteousness with your desires. Let Him feel with your emotions. Let Him choose with your will. Listen for the Spirit's promptings, and yield your members as instruments of righteousness.

It takes time and practice to develop mature discernment, so do not be easily discouraged.

> Heb. 5:14 But solid food belongs to those who are of full age, *that is,* those <u>who by reason of use have their senses exercised to discern both good and evil</u>.

As you learn to discern His voice, surrender to His will, and obey His word in every circumstance of life, you will be caught up into the activity of God.

Your part is to seek the Lord and His kingdom first.

> Col. 3:1 If then you were raised with Christ, <u>seek those things which are above</u>, where Christ is, sitting at the right hand of God.
> Col. 3:2 <u>Set your mind on things above</u>, not on things on the earth.

Do not be distracted or focus on what others are doing or not doing. You are God's workmanship.

> Eph. 2:10   For <u>we are His workmanship, created in Christ Jesus for good works,</u> which God prepared beforehand that we should walk in them.

The word translated *workmanship* (Greek: *poema*) is the origin of our English word *poem*. The implication is unmistakable—you are a unique creation, God's masterpiece, and He has ordained your life and ministry to reveal His glory. As you daily surrender to His will and renew your mind through His word, the Lord Jesus will transform your life. To your delight, you will discover that His will is good not evil, perfect not flawed, and acceptable rather than objectionable, or as Blackaby put it "what you would choose every time if you had all the facts."

> Rom. 12:1   I beseech you therefore, brethren, by the mercies of God, that you <u>present your bodies a living sacrifice,</u> holy, acceptable to God, *which is* your reasonable service.
> Rom. 12:2   And do not be conformed to this world, but <u>be transformed by the renewing of your mind,</u> that you may <u>prove what *is* that good and acceptable and perfect will of God.</u>

The account of Phillip and the Ethiopian Eunuch in Acts 8:26-40 illustrates how simple obedience brings us into the activity of God.

> Acts 8:26   Now <u>an angel of the Lord spoke to Philip, saying, Arise and go toward the south along the road which goes down from Jerusalem to Gaza,</u> This is desert.
> Acts 8:27   <u>So he arose and went.</u> And behold, a man of Ethiopia, a eunuch of great authority under Candace the queen of the Ethiopians, who had charge of all her treasury, and had come to Jerusalem to worship,
>
> Acts 8:29   <u>Then the Spirit said to Philip, Go near and overtake this chariot.</u>
> Acts 8:30   So <u>Philip ran to him, and heard him</u>

73

reading the prophet Isaiah, and said, Do you
understand what you are reading?
Acts 8:31   And he said, How can I, except someone
guides me? And he asked Philip to come up and sit
with him.

Acts 8:35 Then Philip opened his mouth, and
beginning at this scripture, preached Jesus to him.
Acts 8:36 Now as they went down the road, they
came to some water. And the eunuch said, See, *here
is* water. What hinders me from being baptized?
Acts 8:37 Then Philip said, If you believe with all
you heart, you may. And he answered and said, I
believe that Jesus Christ is the Son of God.

Acts 8:39 Now when they came up out of the water,
the Spirit of the Lord caught Philip away, so that the
eunuch saw him no more; and he went on his way
rejoicing.
Acts 8:40 But Philip was found at Azotus. And
passing through, he preached in all the cities till he
came to Caesarea.

Joining Jesus in His activity may be interceding for someone
who is lost, a fellow believer, a Christian leader, or ministry. It
may be praying for those in authority, or pleading with God for
revival and spiritual awakening. It may involve confessing sin,
singing praise to God, preaching or listening to a sermon, studying
your Bible, memorizing a verse, meditating on a Scripture,
witnessing to a lost person, asking forgiveness from an offended
brother or sister, reproving a sinner, restoring a wayward believer,
giving to God's work, attending a Bible conference, preparing a
meal, spending time with your family, visiting a shut-in, calling to
check on a friend—the list is practically endless.

God's activity may be what He is doing in your life or what
He is doing in relation to someone else. Nevertheless, it is simple
obedience that brings us into Jesus' activity. That is how He
joined the Father in His activity and how you and I join Him in His
work.

Like Jesus during His incarnation, we can do nothing of ourselves. However, as we abide in Jesus, i.e., trust our Lord and obey His commandments, He has promised to work His works through us.

> John 15:5 I am the vine, you *are* the branches. He who abides in Me, and I in him, bears much fruit; for without Me you can do nothing.

Indeed, the whole of the Christian life rises or falls on this one issue—obedience—not partial obedience, picking and choosing "buffet style" what we will do and what we will not do. Our obedience to Jesus must be the same obedience that He demonstrated to the Father—complete, total obedience everywhere, all the time, regardless of the circumstances or consequences. Anything less is disobedience, and Jesus will not bless disobedience.

Disobedience is why many Christians experience little joy, meaning, purpose, or power in their lives. Disobedience removes us from the activity of God. Our lives are not *fulfilled* because we are not *fulfilling* our Lord's will. We are not obedient to Jesus the way He was obedient to the Father.

> Ps. 40:8 I delight to do Your will, O my God, and Your law *is* within my heart.

Disobedience is also why many churches are plateaued or declining. As one observer noted, we have shifted our emphasis from being "fishers of men" to "keepers of the aquarium." At great expense spiritually and monetarily, we have decided to focus on maintaining our programs, facilities, and the "status quo" instead of making disciples of the nations as Jesus commanded.

By subordinating the priority to preach the gospel to every creature and focusing instead on providing services to our membership, we have rejected the very basis for kingdom growth and offended the Lord of the Church. Consequently, we do not sense His love because He is not showing us what He is doing and bringing us into His activity. Moreover, because we do not know where Jesus is at work, we are left to our own devices—our programs, initiatives, creativity, innovations, and solutions—to deal with our declining influence. However, you cannot do God's work in man's way or in man's strength. We need God's answers and His power to accomplish His agenda. Nothing else will suffice.

Christianity was birthed in the most backward of circumstances and in the midst of great persecution. Against all odds, it not only survived but thrived and changed the world. We are not facing anything today that Jesus has not anticipated or cannot handle. He promised to build His church in spite of Satan's resistance.

> Mt. 16:18   And I also say to you, that you are Peter, and on this rock I will build My church, and the gates of Hades shall not prevail against it.

However, it is not our determination, skills, and resources that will bring success. To do what Jesus commanded requires Him to work in and through us.

> Mt. 28:18   And Jesus came and spoke to them, saying, All authority has been given to Me in heaven and on earth.
> Mt. 28:19   Go therefore and make disciples of all the nations, baptizing them in the name of the Father, and of the Son, and of the Holy Spirit,
> Mt. 28:20   Teaching them to observe all things that I have commanded you; and, lo, I am with you always, even unto the end of the age. Amen.

Only by His presence and power, expressed though believers individually and the church corporately, can we impact our families, our communities, and this world. I believe that will only happen when we understand our relationship with Jesus and relate to Him as He did to His Father—obeying His commandments, discerning where He is at work, joining Him in His activity, and relying on His power.

Obedience, pure and simple, is the key! It was by His obedience that Jesus remained in the Father's love. Likewise, it is by obedience that we remain in His love.

> John 15:10 If you keep My commandments, you will abide in My love; just as I have kept My Father's commandments and abide in His love.

As we remain (i.e. abide, continue) in Jesus' love by obeying His commandments, He will express His love to us in all the ways the Father expressed His love for the Son.

A beloved hymn captures the simple reality I believe God is looking for *and* what He is prepared to do for each of us.

> "But we never can prove the delights of his love
> Until all on the altar we lay.
> For the favor he shows and the joy he bestows
> Are for them who will trust and obey.

Is there any area of disobedience in your life? Are you becoming more aware of God's activity as you obey Jesus? Is Jesus bringing you into His activity?

12- EXPRESSING HIS LOVE

As we have already seen, God expressed His love for the Son by showing Him what He was doing and bringing Jesus into His activity. However, that was just two of several ways the Father demonstrated His love for the Son. Let's explore them now by asking the question...

How does Jesus express His love to us?

In the days of His flesh, Jesus did not have to guess about the Father's love, and we do not have to wonder about Jesus' love for us. There were practical and tangible evidences of God's love for His Son. The Father expressed His love to Jesus in at least seven ways. As we have seen previously...

* The Father loved the Son by revealing Himself and His activity (Manifestation). Not all at once but progressively, the Father showed the Son what He was doing as Jesus walked in perfect obedience.

> John 5:20 For the Father loves the Son, and shows Him all things that He Himself does: and He will show Him greater works than these, that you may marvel.

Jesus has promised to do the same for us as we walk in simple faith and obedience to Him.

> John 14:21 He who has My commandments, and keeps them, it is he who loves Me. And he who loves Me will be loved by My Father, <u>and I will love him, and manifest Myself to him</u>.

We have also noted previously that...

* God expressed His love for Jesus by bringing Him into His activity (Participation). As the Father revealed His activity to the Son, Jesus simply joined His Father and did whatever He was doing.

> John 5:19 Then Jesus answered and said to them, Most assuredly, I say to you, The Son can do nothing of Himself, but what He sees the Father do: <u>for whatever He does, the Son also does in like manner</u>. John 5:20 <u>For the Father loves the Son</u>, and shows Him all things that He Himself does; and He will show Him greater works than these, that you may marvel.

We also have Jesus' promise that He will bring us into His activity as we believe and obey Him.

> John 14:12 Most assuredly, I say to you, <u>He who believes in Me</u>, the works that I do he will do also; and greater works than these he will do because I go to My Father.

* The Father filled and indwelled the Son as an expression of His love (Habitation).

The Father and the Son express Their love for believers by coming and making Their abode with us.

> John 14:23 Jesus answered and said to him, If anyone loves Me, he will keep My word; <u>and My Father will love him, and We will come to him, and make Our home with him</u>.

79

Since Jesus loves you and me in the same way the Father loved Him, we can infer that the Father filled and indwelt Jesus as an expression of His love for the Son as witnessed at His baptism.

> Mt. 3:16 When He had been baptized, Jesus came up immediately from the water; and behold, the heavens were opened to Him, and He saw the Spirit of God descending like a dove and alighting upon Him.
> Mt. 3:17 And suddenly a voice came from heaven, saying, This is My beloved Son, in whom I am well pleased.
>
> John 3:34 For He whom God has sent speaks the words of God, for God does not give the Spirit by measure (to Him).

* The Father expressed His love for Jesus by giving Him authority and responsibility to do His work. (Delegation)

> John 3:35 The Father loves the Son, and has given all things into His hand.

The miracles that followed Jesus were given to Him by His Father to verify that He came from God.

> John 10:37 If I do not do the works of My Father, do not believe Me.
> John 10:38 But if I do, though you do not believe Me, believe the works, that you may know and believe that the Father is in Me, and I in Him.

Jesus loves us by giving us authority and responsibility to do His work—authority to act in His name, to ask and receive in His name, and to carry out His mission.

> John 17:18 As You sent Me into the world, I also have sent them into the world.

* The Father loved Jesus by acknowledging and affirming Him as His Son (Affirmation),

2 Pet. 1:17 For He received from God the Father honor and glory when such a voice came to Him from the Excellent Glory: "This is My beloved Son, in whom I am well pleased."
2 Pet. 1:18 And we heard this voice which came from heaven when we were with Him on the holy mountain.

Similarly, Jesus expresses His love to us by affirming us and assuring us that we are His. The indwelling Holy Spirit is God's acknowledgement that we belong to Him and the deposit guaranteeing our future inheritance.

1 John 3:1 Behold, what manner of love the Father has bestowed on us, that we should be called children of God! Therefore the world does not know us, because it did not know Him.

Rom. 8:15 For you did not received the spirit of bondage again to fear, but you received the Spirit of adoption by whom we cry out, Abba, Father.
Rom. 8:16 The Spirit Himself bears witness with our spirit that we are children of God:

* The Father expressed His love for Jesus by training and maturing Him (Perfection).

Heb. 5:7 Who, in the days of His flesh, when He had offered up prayers and supplications, with vehement cries and tears to Him who was able to save Him from death, and was heard because of His godly fear,
Heb. 5:8 Though He was a Son, yet He learned obedience by the things which He suffered.
Heb. 5:9 And having been perfected, He became the author of eternal salvation to all who obey Him;

Unlike us, the chastening and training Jesus endured was not because of sin. Still, He had to learn the discipline of obedience through great suffering to become a faithful High Priest. He had to be tested in His will without giving in to sin: to choose between asserting His deity or trusting His Father's care, to choose between doing what He preferred or what the Father commanded, to choose between standing up for Himself or suffering unjustly.

Similarly, Jesus expresses His love for us by chastening, training, and perfecting.

> Heb. 12:6 For whom the Lord loves He chastens, And scourges every son whom He receives.
>
> Rev. 3:19 As many as I love, I rebuke and chasten. Therefore be zealous and repent.

* The Father expressed His love for the Son by vindicating Him (Vindication). The resurrection was God's stamp of approval and the ultimate vindication of the life and ministry of Jesus.

> Rom. 1:4 And declared to be the Son of God with power according to the Spirit of holiness, by the resurrection from the dead:
>
> Phil. 2:9 Therefore God also has highly exalted Him and given Him the name which is above every name:
> Phil. 2:10 That at the name of Jesus every knee should bow, of those in heaven, and those on earth, and those under the earth;
> Phil. 2:11 And that every tongue should confess that Jesus Christ is Lord, to the glory of God the Father.

Likewise, Jesus expresses His love by vindicating His own before a lost and unbelieving world now and when He comes. Daniel, Hananiah, Mishael, and Azariah experienced this expression of God's love as did David, who frequently appealed to God for vindication.

> Ps. 35:1 Plead *my cause*, O LORD, with those who strive with me; fight against those who fight against me.
> Ps. 35:2 Take hold of shield and buckler, and stand up for my help.

Jesus promised vindication to the believers at Philadelphia who were being opposed by Jewish unbelievers.

> Rev. 3:9   Indeed I will make those of the synagogue of Satan, who say they are Jews and are not, but lie —indeed <u>I will make them come and worship before your feet, and to know that I have loved you</u>.

Jesus does not want us to guess and wonder about His love. He loves us as the Father loved Him. So, He gives us practical, tangible expressions of His love just as the Father did for Him.

> John 15:9   <u>As the Father has loved Me, I also have loved you</u>: abide in My love.

As we obey His commandments, we abide (i.e. continue, remain) in a love relationship with Jesus and enjoy the many expressions of His   perfect   love—manifestation,   participation,   habitation, delegation, affirmation, perfection, and vindication.

Do you sometimes wonder about God's love? What does your obedience say about your love for Jesus? Are you remaining in His love by keeping His commandments just as He kept His Fathers' commandments? Is Jesus expressing His love to you in the ways the Father expressed His love for the Son?

13- FROM PRECEPT TO PRACTICE

The kind of obedience, loyalty, and devotion to Jesus we have been discussing is not possible in our human condition. Our best is not good enough. Even after conversion, we cannot of ourselves live the life of faith and produce much fruit that remains.

> John 15:5 I am the vine, you *are* the branches: He who abides in Me, and I in him, bears much fruit: <u>for without Me you can do nothing</u>.

The following question is of paramount importance.

How do we take what we have learned and live in relationship with Jesus as He did with the Father?

If you have grown up in the Protestant tradition, you have been taught that grace (Greek: *karis*) is God's unmerited favor. This understanding of grace likely prevailed as the predominant view among Protestants as a response to the doctrine of salvation by works taught by the Roman Catholic church. You may also have been taught that mercy is God *not giving* me what I deserve, while grace is God *giving me what I don't deserve*. However, is this all the Bible reveals about grace?

James Dunn in his commentary, *Romans 1-8*, wrote, "Grace is never merely an attitude or disposition of God...consistently it denotes something much more *dynamic*...it denotes *effective divine power* in the experience of men." (Emphasis added)

In summarizing the article entitled "Grace," *The International Standard Bible Encyclopedia* states, "Most of the discussions of the Biblical doctrine of grace have been faulty in narrowing the meaning of "grace" to some special sense, and then endeavoring to force this special sense on all the Biblical passages...A rigid definition is hardly possible, but still a single conception is actually present in almost every case where "grace" is found—the conception that all a Christian has or is, is centered exclusively in God and Christ, and depends utterly on God through Christ. The kingdom of heaven is reserved for those who become as little children, for those who look to their Father in loving confidence for every benefit, whether it be for *the pardon so freely given*, or for *the strength that comes from Him who works in them both to will and to do*." (Emphasis added)

Grace is God's favor, and it is unmerited. However, grace has a practical side. It is expressed in a person's life as *the desire and power God gives us to do His will*. Grace describes the supernatural enablement God supplies through His Spirit to accomplish His purposes. Unfortunately, this truth is not widely understood or appreciated by a great many professing Christians. Consequently, God's work suffers because the Father's business is usually done on the basis of human wisdom, ability, and determination.

When Stephen was stoned to death, persecution forced many believers to leave Jerusalem. Some of them went to Antioch in Syria and preached Christ, and a great number of gentiles (non-Jews) believed in Jesus. When news of the revival reached Peter and the remaining disciples in Jerusalem, they sent Barnabas to verify what was happening. In Acts 11:23, we read of Barnabas...

> Acts 11:23 When he came, and <u>had seen the grace of God</u>, he was glad, and encouraged them all that

with purpose of heart they should continue with the
Lord.

What did Barnabas see? How was the grace of God observable to
him? He saw a multitude of people turning from idolatry and
believing in the Jewish Messiah, Jesus. In other words, he saw a
host of new believers filled with the desire and power to do the
will of God.

> Acts 11:21 And the hand of the Lord was with them,
> and <u>a great number believed, and turned to the Lord</u>.

If you asked the apostle Paul the explanation for his
conversion and ministry, *grace* would be his answer.

> 1 Cor. 15:10 But <u>by the grace of God I am what I
> am</u>, and His grace toward me was not in vain; <u>but I
> labored more abundantly than they all, yet not I, but
> the grace of God which was with me</u>.

Paul did not live on the basis of willpower and determination, but
by God's enabling grace—the desire and power He gives us to do
His will.   That was how he lived, ministered, and became the
greatest missionary in church history.

> 2 Cor. 1:12 For our boasting is this: the testimony
> of our conscience that <u>we conducted ourselves in the
> world</u> in simplicity and godly sincerity, not with
> fleshly wisdom but <u>by the grace of God,</u> and more
> abundantly to you.

When Paul wrote to the Corinthians to encourage their giving
for the saints in Jerusalem, he cited God's abounding grace as the
enabling power for every good work.

> 2 Cor. 9:8 And God *is* able to make <u>all grace abound
> toward you, that you</u>, always having all sufficiency in
> all *things*, may <u>have an abundance for (or abound to)
> every good work</u>:

Grace solves two problems we all have without denying our
accountability or violating our freedom of choice. When we don't

want to do the will of God, grace supplies the desire to obey. When we cannot do the will of God, grace supplies the power or ability to obey. Yet, God does not force it upon us. We can accept grace and benefit, or we can reject it and suffer loss.

The Bible describes grace as manifold (Greek: *poikilos-* of various colors, variegated; of various sorts- Thayer).

> 1 Pet. 4:10 As each one has received a gift, minister it to one another, as good stewards of the manifold grace of God.

Manifold grace is diverse, assorted grace—grace suited to every occasion, need, and contingency. Through the indwelling Spirit of grace, God gives us the desire and power to repent and trust Jesus.

> Eph. 2:8 For by grace you have been saved through faith, and that not of yourselves; *it is* the gift of God, Eph. 2:9 Not of works, lest anyone should boast.

We receive grace to give, believe, witness, understand, love, pray, serve, etc.

> 2 Cor. 8:6 So we urged Titus, that as he had begun, so he would also complete this grace in you as well. 2 Cor. 8:7 But as you abound in everything—in faith, in speech, in knowledge, in all diligence, and in your love to us—*see* that you abound in this grace also.

The Holy Spirit also supplies grace for the special trials of life—grace sufficient to resist temptation, to believe in the face of the impossible, to stand when you are all alone, to face death with confidence, and to endure great suffering as with the apostle Paul.

> 2 Cor. 12:7 And lest I should be exalted above measure by the abundance of the revelations, a thorn in the flesh was given to me, a messenger of Satan to buffet me, lest I be exalted above measure. 2 Cor. 12:8 Concerning this thing I pleaded with the

Lord three times, that it might depart from me.
2 Cor. 12:9 And He said to me, <u>My grace is
sufficient for you, for My strength is made perfect in
weakness</u>. Therefore most gladly I will rather boast
in my infirmities, that the power of Christ may rest
upon me.

The only reason we fail in the Christian life is because in our
pride and rebellion, we refuse God's grace to do better. When Paul
faced the challenges of ministry and living with personal infirmity,
he did not resist God's grace. He did what the writer of Hebrews
admonished...

> Heb. 4:16 Let us therefore come boldly to the throne
> of grace, that we may obtain mercy <u>and find grace to
> help in time of need</u>.

When Paul humbled himself under God's mighty hand, he
discovered for himself just what Jesus promised: "My grace is
sufficient for you."

In reality, God never intended for us to live our lives in our
own strength. If we did, we could boast: *See how many people I
led to Christ. See how many churches I planted. Look how my
church has grown under my leadership. Look at how much we
gave to missions.* However, God intends for us to live on the basis
of grace—the desire and power He supplies—that "no flesh should
glory in His presence." He deliberately chooses what man
disregards that He might demonstrate His glory.

> 1 Cor. 1:27 But God has chosen the <u>foolish things</u>
> of the world to put to shame the wise, and God has
> chosen the <u>weak things</u> of the world to put to shame
> the things which are mighty;
> 1 Cor. 1:28 And the <u>base things</u> of the world and the
> the <u>things which are despised</u> God has chosen, and
> the <u>things which are not</u>, to bring to nothing the
> things that are,
> 1 Cor. 1:29 <u>That no flesh should glory in His
> presence</u>.

God has fresh supplies of grace for every day and every need we face.

> 2 Cor. 9:8 And God *is* able to make all (every) grace abound toward you, that you, always having all sufficiency in all *things*, may have an abundance for (or abound to) every good work:

To receive His grace, all we need to do is look to Jesus. The psalmist wrote of the coming Messiah...

> Ps. 45:2 You are fairer than the sons of men; grace is poured upon Your lips; Therefore God has blessed You forever.

In describing Jesus, John wrote...

> John 1:14 And the Word became flesh and dwelt among us, and we beheld His glory, the glory as of the only begotten of the Father, full of grace and truth.

Furthermore, we are the recipients and beneficiaries of His grace.

> John 1:16 And of His fullness we have all received, and grace for grace (i.e. grace upon grace).
> John 1:17 For the law was given through Moses, *but* grace and truth came through Jesus Christ.

The grace that was fully present in Jesus, evident in the believers at Antioch, and powerfully at work in the apostle Paul is available to you and me when we humble ourselves under God's mighty hand and ask for it.

> James 4:6 But He gives more grace. Therefore He says: God resists the proud, but gives grace to the humble.

God hates pride in any form. It was the root cause of Satan's rebellion and subsequent judgment. It makes God our enemy, and robs us of His grace. However, the High and Holy God who inhabits eternity loves and dwells with those who are of a broken and contrite heart.

> Isa. 57:15 For thus says the High and Lofty One who inhabits eternity, whose name *is* Holy: "I dwell in the high and holy *place*, with him *who* has a contrite and humble spirit, to revive the spirit of the humble, and to revive the heart of the contrite ones.

Finally, since grace is real and practical, it can be refused and resisted. Paul chided the Galatians not that they had lost their salvation, but they had ceased to consciously rely on God's provision of righteousness through faith in Jesus.

> Gal. 5:1 Stand fast therefore in the liberty by which Christ has made us free, and do not be entangled again with a yoke of bondage.
> Gal. 5:2 Indeed I, Paul, say to you that if you become circumcised, Christ will profit you nothing.
> Gal. 5:3 And I testify again to every man who becomes circumcised that he is a debtor to keep the whole law.
> Gal. 5:4 You have become estranged from Christ, you who *attempt to* be justified by law; you have fallen from grace.

There are only two ways to relate to God. Either we trust what Jesus did for us, or we depend on what we can do for ourselves. It is the classic struggle of faith versus works—of relying on the righteousness of Jesus or depending on our own human goodness and good deeds. By ceasing to exercise the grace of faith (the desire and power God gives us to believe) and returning to the self-righteousness that comes from keeping the law, the Galatian believers had fallen from grace.

In reality, it is very easy to fail of the grace of God. It happens naturally every time we try to do God's will in our own strength or ability. When we refuse to admit we need help and hang on to our pride and self-sufficiency, we fail of the grace of God. When we trust our education, training, and abilities to accomplish God's purposes, we fall from grace. When we live every day on the basis of grit and determination doing "the best we can," we refuse and resist the grace of God. Moreover, without the desire and power God supplies to do His will, we miss out on what He can do, and we are forced to settle for the best we can do.

The Holy Spirit is a person. He can be grieved, and His activity in our lives can be quenched.

> Eph. 4:30 And do not grieve the Holy Spirit of God, by whom you were sealed for the day of redemption.
>
> 1 Thess. 5:19 Do not quench the Spirit.

When we refuse His grace and minister in our own strength and abilities, we insult the Spirit of God and shut down His work in our lives. I believe what I have just described happens every Sunday in the average church. We go through the motions of worship. We have a bulletin that tells us what is going to happen in the service. We have our music and Bible Study programs to bolster our feelings and increase our knowledge, but God rarely shows up. Little happens that we cannot explain in terms of human personality, motivation, and manipulation.

Monday through Saturday is not much different. The word of God sown in our hearts on Sunday is choked by cares and riches and pleasures of this life, and we struggle to bring any fruit to maturity. The world squeezes us into its mold, and we are unable to prove God's good, perfect, and acceptable will for ourselves or anyone else. *Failing of the grace of God becomes the norm.* We cease to have any impact on our world. In our hearts, we know better, but we struggle to find the desire or the power for lasting change. Our supply of grace runs low because we are not staying connected to Jesus, the Source of grace, and we are not yielding to the Spirit of grace.

Friend, grace works! It is not just an attitude or disposition of God. It is effective, divine power in our experience. It is not just unmerited favor. It is also the strength that comes from Him who works in us "both to will and to do His good pleasure." Willpower, determination, and resolve will fail when the path is rough and the way is steep, but God's grace is always sufficient.

Are you daily finding grace sufficient for every need—grace to give, to witness, to pray, to serve, to resist temptation, to believe in the face of the impossible, to stand when you are all alone, to endure great suffering, or to face death with confidence? Is there anything happening in your life that cannot be explained apart from God? Has failing of the grace of God become the norm in your experience?

14- HONORING THE SON

There is one final question that begs to be asked.

How should we respond to what God is saying?

To experience the relationship with His Son that God intends for us, it is not enough to invite Jesus into your heart and ask Him to save you from your sins. That is just the first step of obedience in a life of total surrender to His Lordship. To be rightly related to Jesus, we must be devoted to Him as He was devoted to the Father. For this to happen, we must reject a nominal Christian experience and choose to receive the abundance of grace that is in Messiah Jesus.

I believe this is what the apostle had in mind when he used the phrase "the grace of life" in 1 Peter 3.

> 1 Pet. 3:7 Husbands, likewise, dwell with *them* with understanding, giving honor to the wife, as to the weaker vessel, and as *being* heirs together of the grace of life, that your prayers may not be hindered.

As we have shown previously, there are all kinds of grace— grace to repent, believe, understand, love, pray, witness, give,

93

serve, stand, suffer, endure, etc. One of those assorted graces is *the grace of life*. The grace of life *is* God's unmerited favor in giving us eternal life through His Son, but it is also *the gracious expression of that life*—the very life of Jesus—in and through us every day. It is the desire and power God gives us to live a life of joy and victory right here, right now. It is the divine enablement to live life to the fullest, to live the life of heaven on earth, to experience the abundant life of Christ.

> John 10:10 The thief does not come except to steal, and to kill, and to destroy. <u>I have come that they may have life, and that they may have *it* more abundantly</u>.

The grace of life is not just believing there is a God, but having a personal relationship with God.

- It is not being frustrated and wounded by the disappointments of life, but reigning in life.
- It is not being confused about life choices, but having the guidance of the Holy Spirit in your decisions.
- It is not just choosing a career, but discovering God's unique plan and purpose for your life.
- It is not marrying the man or woman of your dreams, but daily delighting in your spouse and experiencing the joy and oneness God intended in marriage.
- It is not settling for a roof over your head, but having a home where Christ is honored.
- It is not being satisfied to raise children who are well educated and successful, but raising sons and daughters who know and love Jesus.
- It is not settling for material success, but seeking those things that money cannot buy, time cannot tarnish, and death cannot take away.
- It is facing trials and tribulations with confident expectation rather than bitter cynicism, knowing that God is working all things together for your good.
- It is not just surviving life, but being an overcomer.

The grace of life means coming to the end of your days not uncertain about eternity but confident like Paul, rejoicing, ready to meet your Maker knowing that nothing can separate us from the love of Christ—not tribulation, or distress, or persecution, or famine, or nakedness, or peril, or sword. It is being a "super conqueror" and being fully persuaded that nothing—not death nor life, nor angels, nor principalities, nor powers, nor things present, nor things to come, nor height, nor depth, nor any other created thing, shall be able to separate us from the love of God which is in Christ Jesus our Lord.

The abundant life, the life of faith and victory that joins God in His activity and works His works, is only possible when we are rightly related to Jesus. Bible study, preaching, prayer, worship, evangelism, ministry, missions, etc., are *not* the relationship. They can be and often are substitutes, but they are properly the outgrowth and overflow of our relationship with Jesus. They can even be done in the absence of a healthy relationship to Christ. The scribes and Pharisees worshipped the true God, studied the Scriptures, loved to pray on the street corners, taught the Word of God, compassed land and sea to make a convert, and ministered to the people, but did so while rejecting God's Son.

Nothing of eternal value and duration are possible without Jesus. All God's purposes in Creation, Redemption, Subjugation, and Consummation are centered in His Son. God has determined that in all things, Christ must be preeminent. Therefore, *we must have a personal, particular, and passionate devotion to Jesus.*

When Jesus came among us, He came in His Father's name, acting as His agent and doing His will. He revealed the Father by perfectly embodying the character of the One who sent Him. Jesus fulfilled the prophecies of God, revealed the ways of God, and worked the works of God. In the days of His flesh, He was God's Prophet speaking all that the Father commanded Him. As the only mediator between God and men, Jesus presently ministers as our Great High Priest in the heavenly Tabernacle. Soon He will return as King of all Kings and Lord of all Lords. *There can be no middle ground when it comes to Jesus.*

95

* Only Jesus has seen and knows the Father.

> John 6:46 Not that anyone has seen the Father, except He who is from God, He has seen the Father.

> John 7:29 But I know Him: for I am from Him, and He sent Me.

* Knowing the Father is impossible apart from Jesus.

> Mt. 11:27 All things have been delivered to Me by My Father, and no one knows the Son except the Father. Nor does anyone know the Father except the Son, and *the one* to whom the Son wills to reveal *Him.*

* To see Jesus is to see the Father, and to believe on Jesus is to believe on the Father.

> John 12:44 Then Jesus cried out and said, He who believes in Me, believes not in Me but in Him who sent Me.
> John 12:45 And he who sees Me sees Him who sent Me.

* Moreover, Jesus is the only way to the Father.

> John 14:6 Jesus said to him, I am the way, the truth, and the life. No one comes to the Father except through Me.

We must have an intimate relationship with Jesus modeled after His relationship with the Father. Our passion must be intimacy with, empowerment by, and identification with Jesus.

> Phil. 3:10 That I may know Him and the power of His resurrection, and the fellowship of His sufferings, being conformed to His death,

* Christ must be our life.

> Phil. 1:21 For to me, to live *is* Christ, and to die *is* gain.

* Doing His will must be our food.

> John 4:34   Jesus said to them, "My food is to do the
> will of Him who sent Me, and to finish His work.

* Absolutely nothing can eclipse our devotion to Jesus.

> Lk. 14:26   If anyone comes to Me <u>and does not hate
> his father and mother, wife and children, brothers
> and sisters, yes, and his own life also</u>, he cannot be
> My disciple.

* As Jesus was one with the Father, we must be one with Jesus.

> John 17:13   Now I am no longer in the world, but
> these are in the world, and I come to You. Holy
> Father, keep through Your name those whom You
> have given Me, <u>that they may be one as We *are*</u>.

* We must honor and serve Jesus.

> John 12:26   <u>If anyone serves Me, let him follow
> Me</u>; and where I am, there My servant will be also.
> <u>If anyone serves Me, him *My* Father will honor</u>.

* He must be the object and focus of our faith.

> John 6:28   Then they said to Him, <u>What shall we
> do, that we may work the works of God?</u>
> John 6:29   Jesus answered and said to them, <u>This
> is the work of God, that you believe in Him whom
> He sent</u>.

> John 14:1   Let not your heart be troubled; you
> believe in God, <u>believe also in Me</u>.

* We must exalt Jesus.

> John 12:32   <u>And I, if I am lifted up from the earth,
> will draw all *peoples* to Myself</u>..

* Jesus must be preeminent in all we say and do.

> Col. 1:18 And He is the head of the body, the church, who is the beginning, the firstborn from the dead, <u>that in all things He may have the preeminence</u>.

As my friend, Pastor Matt Buckles, would say, "It must be Christ first, Christ only, and Christ always."

Are you experiencing the grace of life that is only possible through God's Son? Do you have a personal relationship with Jesus modeled after His relationship with the Father? Is your passion to be intimate with Jesus, empowered by Jesus, and identified with Jesus?

15- SUMMARY & CONCLUSION

The Bible teaches that God's will for every believer is to be one with His Son and to join Jesus in His activity in this world. This is the Father's will for you and for me. For this to happen, I am convinced that we must understand and embrace the following truths presented in this brief work:

The Christian faith is not a religion but a relationship. Relationship is God's idea, and it is fundamental to who He is. Moreover, He desires a relationship with us that is real and personal. He wants us to know and experience Him.

By definition, a relationship has many dimensions—accessibility, communication, intimacy, love, fellowship, appreciation, responsibility, trust, and transparency. Jesus has promised to be to us all that a relationship implies.

To begin a relationship with Jesus we must repent of our sins and receive Him as Savior and Lord of our lives. Going forward, we prove that we are truly His disciples through a life of deepening faith and obedience to His commandments.

Through His Son, God has provided all that is necessary for us to be rightly related to Him. Jesus is our advocate. He is the propitiation for our sins and our righteousness. Sin cannot destroy our relationship, but it will break our fellowship with Jesus. To remain rightly related to our Lord, we must deal with sin and iniquity as it occurs.

Jesus did not assert His deity to accomplish His mission. All that He said and did was as the Son of man relying on His heavenly Father. By always obeying the Father, He remained in the Father's love. The Father expressed His love to the Son by showing Jesus all that He was doing and bringing Him into His activity.

Jesus described His relationship to the Father and our relationship to Him in the same terms, indicating that when we are born again, we are placed in the same relationship with Jesus that He enjoyed with His Father. Eternal life is knowing and being known of God. This is what we were made for, and it is the only way we can enjoy true meaning and purpose in life.

The Holy Spirit is the third person of the Trinity, possessing all the attributes of deity. Through the Holy Spirit, Jesus comes to us, indwells us, and enables us to continue His work. The Spirit of grace supplies both the desire and power to do whatever Jesus commands. To fully manifest the life of Christ in our mortal bodies, we must be completely surrendered to the Spirit of God.

Since returning to the Father, Jesus exercises all the prerogatives of deity. He hears and answers prayer offered to the Father in His name. As the exalted God-Man, Jesus has lifted us into the presence of God where *in Christ* we have been graciously endowed with all the privileges of Son-ship. Now, empowered by His Spirit, we can continue His mission.

As the resurrected, ascended Lord, Jesus has promised to do whatever we ask in His name. However, this privilege is reserved for those who know Jesus, those who are abiding in Jesus, and those who are carrying out His work and agenda.

We must understand that prayer "in Jesus' name" is not a magic formula. Fundamentally, it is acting as His agent and asking in His stead. Moreover, it implies that we are rightly related to Jesus, that our prayer is in harmony with God's ways, God's will, and God's timing, that we are asking with Jesus' authority, that our aim is God's glory, and that we are asking on the basis of Jesus' redemption.

Obedience is the way we express our love to Jesus, and He expresses His love to us by revealing Himself and what He is doing. Since obedience is what brings us into the activity of God, we must cultivate the habit of listening for His voice and yielding to His promptings. Our obedience to Jesus must be total obedience—everywhere, always, regardless of the circumstances or cost.

As Jesus walked in perfect obedience, the Father expressed His love for the Son by revealing Himself, by bringing Jesus into His activity, by filling and indwelling the Son, by giving Jesus authority and responsibility to do His work, by acknowledging His Son, by training Him, and by vindicating Jesus before the world. As we obey Jesus, He will love us in all the ways the Father loved Him.

The kind of obedience God requires is impossible apart from grace (i.e. the desire and power God gives us to do His will). Grace is described as manifold, and there is grace for every need—to repent, believe, give, witness, understand, love, pray, serve, etc. Failure in the Christian life can only be attributed to our refusal of grace. Abundance of grace is ours when we daily come to God's throne of grace and ask. Willpower and determination will fail us, but God's grace is always sufficient.

To be rightly related to Jesus, we must be devoted to the Son as He was devoted to the Father. All of God's glorious purposes are centered in Jesus the Messiah. Therefore, we must have a personal, particular, and passionate relationship with Jesus. Our watchword must be Christ first, only, and always.

Going deeper in our relationship with Jesus is not optional, but imperative. It is incumbent upon every Christian to seek the Lord while He may be found and to call upon Him while He is near."

The Word of God commands us to make our calling and election sure and grow in the grace and knowledge of Christ—to add to our faith virtue, to virtue knowledge, to knowledge self-control, to self-control perseverance, to perseverance godliness, to godliness brotherly kindness, and to brotherly kindness love. If we have been raised with Christ, we are to seek those things which are above and work out our salvation with fear and trembling. Like Paul, we must daily press toward the goal of the high calling of God in Christ Jesus.

Time is a non-renewable resource, and some of us have less remaining than others. Therefore, I beseech you as Paul admonished the believers at Corinth that you receive not the grace of God in vain. In the enduring classic, *My Utmost For His Highest,* Oswald Chambers stated,

> "It is not a question of praying and asking God to help you—it is taking the grace of God *now*... The primary word in the spiritual vocabulary is *now*. Let circumstances take you where they will, but keep drawing on the grace of God in whatever condition you may find yourself...Never hold anything in reserve." (Emphasis added)

Don't wait, do it now!

> John 1:16 And of His fullness we have all received, and grace for (upon) grace.
> John 1:17 For the law was given through Moses, *but* grace and truth came through Jesus Christ.

May God use the truth presented in this volume to lead you into a deeper experience of the abundant life that results from being rightly related to Jesus.

SCRIPTURE INDEX

1- RELATIONSHIP

2- DIMESIONS OF RELATIONSHIP

3- GETTING STARTED

4- ROUTINE MAINTENANCE

Pg. 23 - 1 John 1:8, 10; Ex. 20:3-4, 7
Pg. 24 - Ex. 20:8, 12-17; Ps. 32:5; 51:2; Isa. 53:6
Pg. 25 - Ps. 119:2-3
Pg. 26 - 1 John 2:16; Gen. 3:6; Mt. 4:3, 5-6, 8-9
Pg. 27 - 1 John 2:15; 2:1; 2:2
Pg. 28 - Isa. 53:10-11; Heb. 10:12-14; Isa. 53:5-6
Pg. 29 - Rom. 3:21-22; John 10:27-30
Pg. 30 - 1 John 1:7, 9, 10
Pg. 31 - Ps. 32:3-4; 51:3-4

5- OMNISCIENCE OR OBEDIENCE

Pg. 32 - John 11:41-44
Pg. 33 - John 11:4; 5:19; 14:10; 7:16; 8:26-27
Pg. 34 - John 8:28; 12:49-50; 11:20-21; Mk. 6:4-5
Pg. 35 - Mk. 13:32; Rom. 15:2-3; Lk. 23:46; John 5:19; 14:10
Pg. 36 - John 15:10; 5:20; 10:30; 5:17
Pg. 37 - John 15:5

6- THE ABUNDANT LIFE

Pg. 38 - John 14:11; 15:4
Pg. 39 - John 10:29-30; 17:22; 15:9, 10; 5:20; 14:21; 8:42
Pg. 40 - John 20:21; 5:19; 15:5; 9:4; 14:12; 14:10, 12
Pg. 41 - John 14:13-14; Ps. 2:7-9; Rev. 2:26-27; 3:21
Pg. 42 - John 10:10

7- THE OTHER COMFORTER

Pg. 43 - Acts 5:3-4
Pg. 44 - Ps. 139:7-10; 1 Cor. 2:9-11; Heb. 9:13-14
Pg. 45 - John 14:16-18, 23, 26; Zech. 12:10
Pg. 46 - Mt. 28:18-20; John 15:26; 16:13
Pg. 47 - 2 Cor. 4:7-10; Lk. 24:49

8- A NEW PARADIGM

Pg. 49 - Heb. 5:8
Pg. 50 - John 16:16, 23-24, 26, 27; 20:17
Pg. 51 - John 17:9, 11; 14:12, 13-14
Pg. 52 - John 16:22-24
Pg. 53 - 1 John 3:1; Eph. 1:15-19

9- ASKING AND RECEIVING

Pg. 55 - John 14:13-14; 14:12; 15:7
Pg. 56 - John 15:16; James 4:3; Phil. 4:19; John 15:7-8
Pg. 57 - John 15:16; Mt. 28:19-20
Pg. 58 - John 14:12-14; 1 John 5:14-15
Pg. 59 - John 15:5, 7

10- PRAYER IN JESUS' NAME

Pg. 62 - Mt. 21:8-9; Ps. 118:26; Mt. 23:39
Pg. 63 - Mt. 3:16-17; Isa. 55:8; Gal. 1:4
Pg. 64 - Gal. 4:4-5; John 5:43; 1:14; Mt. 20:28
Pg. 65 - Mt. 6:9; 1 John 1:8
Pg. 66 - Ps. 66:18; 1 John 1:9; 5:14
Pg. 67 - Ps. 32:6; Isa. 55:6; Ps. 39:13; 2 Cor. 6:2

11- JOINING JESUS

Pg. 70 - Acts 17:30; John 17:17
Pg. 71 - John 7:16-17; 14:21; Rom. 6:13
Pg. 72 - John 10:27; Heb. 5:14; Col. 3:1-2
Pg. 73 - Eph. 2:10; Rom. 12:1-2; Acts 8:26-27, 29-30
Pg. 74 - Acts 8:31, 35-37, 39-40
Pg. 75 - John 15:5; Ps. 40:8
Pg. 76 - Mt. 16:18; 28:18-20
Pg. 77 - John 15:10

12- EXPRESSING HIS LOVE

Pg. 78 - John 5:20
Pg. 79 - John 14:21; 5:19-20; 14:12, 23
Pg. 80 - Mt. 3:16-17; John 3:34, 35; 10:37-38; 17:18
Pg. 81 - Mt. 3:16-17; 1 John 3:1; Rom. 8:15-16; Heb. 5:7-9
Pg. 82 - Heb. 12:6; Rev. 3:19; Rom. 1:4; Phil. 2:9-11; Ps. 35:1
Pg. 83 - Ps. 35:2; Rev. 3:9; John 15:9

13- FROM PRECEPT TO PRACTICE

Pg. 84 - John 15:5
Pg. 85 - Acts 11:23
Pg. 86 - Acts 11:21; 1 Cor. 15:10; 2 Cor. 1:12; 9:8
Pg. 87 - 1 Pet. 4:10; Eph. 2:8-9; 2 Cor. 8:6-7; 12:7-8
Pg. 88 - 2 Cor. 12:9; Heb. 4:16; 1 Cor. 1:27-29
Pg. 89 - 2 Cor. 9:8; Ps. 45:2; John 1:14, 16-17; James 4:6
Pg. 90 - Isa. 57:15; Gal. 5:1-4

14- HONORING THE SON

Pg. 93 - 1 Pet. 3:7
Pg. 94 - John 10:10
Pg. 96 - John 6:46; 7:29; Mt. 11:27; John 12:44-45; 14:6;
    Phil. 3:10; 1:21;
Pg. 97 - John 4:34; Lk. 14:26; John 17:13; 12:26; 6:28-29; 14:1; 12
    12:32
Pg. 98 - Col. 1:18

15- CONCLUSION

Pg. 102 - John 1:16-17

ABOUT THE AUTHOR

Joel R. Stroud is a Southern Baptist pastor, living in Lyon, MS where he has served Lyon Baptist Church since August of 1989. His spiritual upbringing was in rural churches of Mississippi, Alabama, Georgia, and Florida, served by his father, Daniel W. Stroud, Sr., a bi-vocational pastor and educator. In 1975 while teaching Bible and coaching in Memphis, TN, he met and married his wife and best friend, Sheri. They have one son, Joel Seth, a singer/songwriter living in Clarksdale, MS. Pastor Stroud is a graduate of Delta State University and New Orleans Baptist Theological Seminary. Before coming to Lyon, he served for three and a half years as pastor of Silver Springs Baptist Church near Progress, MS.

Other works by the author:

Thinking His Thoughts: Renewing Your Mind Through Daily Meditation In The Psalms & Proverbs; 299 pg. book.

Discipleship According To Jesus: A Concise Survey Of The Requirements And Implications Of Discipleship; 24 pg. booklet.

No Greater Work: Essays On Effective Prayer; 54 pg. booklet.

A Nation In Need Of Healing: Answering the age old question, "If the foundations be destroyed, what can the righteous do?" Psalm 11:3; 18 pg. booklet.

Disasters: Why? God's Perspective On Hurricanes, Earthquakes, And Other Calamities, 18 pg. booklet.

Contact the author at joelrstroud@gmail.com.